MIMESIS
INTERNATIONAL

C000098517

ASIAN PHILOSOPHICAL TEXTS

No. 2

Book series edited by Roman Paşca (Kyoto University, Japan) and Takeshi Morisato (Sun Yat-Sen University, China)

Editorial Board

Pierre Bonneels (Université libre de Bruxelles, Belgium), Raquel Bouso (University of Pompeu Fabra, Spain), Margaret Chu (The Royal Commonwealth Society in Hong Kong, Hong Kong), Maitreyee Datta (Jadavpur University, India), Yasuo Deguchi (Kyoto University, Japan), Jonardon Ganeri (New York University, USA), Marcello Ghilardi (University of Padova, Italy), Leigh Jenco (London School of Economics and Political Science), Kevin Lam (Dokkyo University, Japan), Ethan Mills (University of Tennessee Chattanooga, USA), Eric Nelson (Hong Kong University of Science and Technology, Hong Kong), Kenn Nakata-Steffensen (University College Dublin, Ireland), Jin Y. Park (American University, USA), Jana Rošker (University of Ljubljana, Slovenia), Shalini Sinha (University of Reading, UK), Andrew Whitehead (Kennesaw State University, USA; KU Leuven, Université libre de Bruxelles, Belgium)

MIMESIS

Tatsuya Higaki

NISHIDA KITARŌ'S PHILOSOPHY OF LIFE

Translated by Jimmy Aames

MIMESIS
INTERNATIONAL

The translation of this book was financially supported by the Osaka University Project for the Dissemination of Research Findings in the Humanities and Social Sciences.

© 2020 – MIMESIS INTERNATIONAL – MILAN
www.mimesisinternational.com
e-mail: info@mimesisinternational.com

Isbn: 9788869772689
Book series: *Asian Philosophical Texts*, n. 2

© MIM Edizioni Srl
P.I. C.F. 02419370305

CONTENTS

SUPPLEMENTARY ESSAYS

JOHN C. MARALDO

FOREWORD

In *Nishida Kitarō's Philosophy of Life*, Tatsuya Higaki takes an uncommonly fresh approach to the most significant Japanese philosopher of the twentieth century. Up to now, presentations of Nishida, particularly in English and other European languages, have attempted variously to frame his work in the context of Japanese modernism and nationalism, or understand it as a Zen Buddhist or East Asian response to Western philosophy, a counterpart to German dialectical thought and to Heideggerian thinking, a resource for current inter-religious and cross-cultural dialogue, or—in my own case—as a challenge to phenomenological metaphysics that takes nothingness as its open-ended foundation. The massive literature on Nishida's thought in Japanese is more varied yet, and includes attempts like Yūjiro Naka-mura's to present it in the context of post-modernism and deconstruc-tion. But nowhere else will we find a sustained treatment that depicts, in fine detail, Nishida's contribution to the international current of thought known as *Lebensphilosophie*, the group of philosophies that present life in its dynamic actuality that can never be captured by the concepts and categories of scientific reason or logic alone. In a broad sense, this vital tradition includes the writings of Friedrich Nietzsche and Henri Bergson, as well as the treatises of Wilhelm Dilthey, Georg Simmel, Hans Driesch, and others. Higaki aptly focuses on the stream of life-philosophy closest to Nishida's evolving thinking: Bergson's presentation of the immediacy of experience and Gilles Deleuze's development of the multiple and virtual actualizing forms it takes. What is more, Higaki shows that Nishida's frequent recourse to mathematical models works with, rather than against, a philosophy of life ever in flow. This book brings these currents—Nishida's, Bergson's, and Deleuze's life-philosophy and mathematics—into contact with one another in a way that augments the force of their insights but also makes visible their occasional dead-ends.

The recurrent theme of the book you are reading may be expressed as a single, fundamental problem: If all reality is a flow—or better said, to avoid the rigidity of the noun—is perpetually flowing, then how is it possible to come to experience and to know this reality? For this reality includes us, our conceptualizations, our actions, our very lives. We do not live outside it; how could we stop it long enough to discern that it, that we, are perpetually in flow? But Nishida's writing rarely expresses this problem in these exact terms. Rather, the author Higaki and we readers must take pains to tease it out of the multiple ways it is intimated in Nishida's repetitious, slowing progressing works that give the impression the problem and its solution remain virtual, waiting to be stated in a definitive formulation. It is as if Nishida's philosophy itself is an example of the impossibility of encapsulating life and what we call reality. Ueda Shizuteru points out that Nishida's first major work, *An Inquiry Into the Good*, went to the root of philosophical explanation in three steps: it attempted to "explain everything on the basis of pure experience as the sole reality," which entails a textual explanation based on the primary sentence, "pure experience [is] the sole reality," where that sentence itself is rooted in the primal or proto-word, "pure experience." But Nishida did not, could not, stop with this three-fold formulation, for the development of this explanation ran into problems that were insolvable in its terms and required a turn in a different direction. The specific issues Nishida encountered along the way, and the various, consecutive turns that he took in presenting the flow of reality, are what the present book is about.

We encounter one intriguing instance of Nishida's multiple "takes" on life, and the problem its explanation elicits, in a passage he wrote in 1933 about forms of poetry—the more experiential form of the Japanese short poem or *tanka* in contrast with the more conceptual short poems of the West. As translated by Michiko Yusa, Nishida writes:

In his *Creative Evolution*, Henri Bergson advanced his view that everything from animal life to plant life and even material movement are but various modes of the vital force (*élan vital*) that unfolds by piercing through the material crust; in this regard, he describes human life as the great emanation of this life force.[1]

Clearly this comment shows Nishida's admiration of the French philosopher's idea. A little later in his brief, impromptu essay, Nishida makes a remark about the form of poetry that best expresses one's life-experience, and that remark puts an interesting twist on the earlier comment and hints at a problem it poses:

To grasp life-experience by way of short poetic form ("*tanshi*") is to grasp it from the center of the present moment. It is to view life from the very moment of experience. Life, surely, is one whole unity, but in grasping this concrete and vibrant life, it is one thing to look at it from the environment; it is quite another to grasp it at the very tip of a vividly pulsating life. Depending on which angle we take to view life, it presents a different vista, and we actually live out a different significance of life.

What Bergson's view of life fails to note, this remark intimates, is the stance that makes possible an understanding or grasp of life as an emanation of the *élan vital*. And that grasp takes place, as it were, at the tip or crest of a pulsating wave at the very moment of experiencing it, in the present moment, from which emanates the flow of experience. But then again we may ask, in retrospect of this remark, what is the nature of the moment that apparently allows it to diverge from the infinite flow of time long enough to grasp the flow precisely as a flow?

This conceptual question is but one instance of the central problem that, for Higaki, drives Nishida's life-philosophy. Higaki is a master at problematizing a lifelong development that only Nishida's death could bring to an end. During his lifetime, Nishida moved through several configurations of the problem, and coined different terminologies, in progressive attempts not so much to solve the problem, once and for all, as rather to express it in a manner that did justice to the infinite movement of life. He began with a conception of the developing whole of reality as a straightforward expansion of the present, but then faced the difficulty that such a view tended to reify (or hyposta-

---

1   Cited in Appendix 2, "On Japanese Short Poetry, 'Tanka' (January 1933)," in Michiko Yusa, ed, *The Bloomsbury Research Handbook of Contemporary Japanese Philosophy*, (London & New York: Bloomsbury, 2017), 366 & 368. The original text is in 11, 162–164. Translation slightly modified.

tize) the infinite by taking all time as mere repetition of the same, an identity that bypassed the differences life presents. Next, he conceived of the infinite as a set of relationships by turning to Richard Dedekind's definition of infinite systems. The relationship of whole to part (for example, of the whole set of natural numbers 1, 2, 3, 4, 5... to the subset of odd numbers 1, 3, 5...) allows for the difference between the sets but maintains the infinity of each. Again, adapting Josiah Royce's version, Nishida imagines the activity of drawing an exact map of the area wherein one is standing, as if to picture the infinite flow of life from within it, from a present that is three-dimensional or spherical. Nishida began to "factorialize" the basic relationship, dividing it into parts each of which mirrors the whole, to express a way that the imagining, active self does not need to stand outside the whole to envision it; the whole reflects itself, "knows" itself, in the part that we call consciousness. Nishida's famed "logic of place" was the result of this attempt to express how the infinity of life and reality is reflected in each "part" or embedded "place" of our progressive knowledge. In the first place, judgments not only predicate something universal of their subjects but reflect the more inclusive consciousness that acts in making judgments; in the second place, consciousness not only takes judgments as prospective candidates for establishing objective truth about the world but also reflects the "intelligible world" that works through it; and in the third place this still more inclusive, intelligible dimension of world or reality not only allows for discovery of truth about it but in fact realizes truth—insofar as truth means the totality of what is. And this totality of reality, ever realizing itself, goes on and on. But then how can any statement at all, any "take" at all on this infinite reality, even begin to approximate the whole of it? Such an infinite whole could be approximated only by taking it as a limit, something like a differential limit of infinitesimal differences. But then this limit could not really be "something" that itself could be surpassed by a different function that has no limit. And so it must expressed as nothing, an absolute nothingness that, to be sure, envelops and is reflected by every relative something. That is to say, absolute nothingness expresses the final emplacement of every thing and every judgment in the infinite reality that includes us. Absolute nothingness reflecting itself in all things turns out to be what actually counts as the first and final place.

These difficult thoughts, which I emphasize are formulated in my own words, are meant to illustrate how Higaki's analysis helped me for one to envision Nishida's progressive placing of an infinite world in mathematical terms. For other readers, Higaki's mathematical explanations may elicit other formulations, none of which will totally capture Nishida's manifold or even Higaki's take on it.

And still, Nishida's philosophy does not rest at this point. Higaki shows how Tanabe Hajime, Nishida's younger colleague and successor, pointed out another kind of limitation to his theory of place—how in postulating a limit to the flow of a reality so as to ensure a place for its infinitude, Nishida ran the danger of making nothingness transcendent to relationships, thus hypostatizing nothingness and, in the end, actually setting it apart and annulling the inherent, dynamic movement of reality. Nishida responded not by abandoning his theory but by conceiving the relation between whole and part as a contradictory self-identity. The whole negates itself in the part and the part negates itself in their mutual enactment, forming a reality ever in becoming. To state the matter again in my own terms, our own place in this reality is assured through "acting intuition"—our performative intuition through which we interact with all things and by which we in turn are formed. At this point in Nishida's development, one might ask again whether our identity, the identity of each of us, is set long enough for a grasp of the whole of infinite ever-flowing reality to occur.

The delightful surprise in Higaki's account is twofold: the profusion of parallels he sights between Nishida's problematic and Bergson's attempt to grasp the infinite flow of life, and the clarifications offered by Deleuze's development of Bergson. A single example of each may serve to entice the reader. Bergson conceives of the "vast and multi-layered reality that encompasses and envelops the present (and its organic relationships)" as "pure memory," and this conception is structurally parallel to Nishida's theory of place and can further elucidate it. Deleuze replaces the notion of *possible* or *potential*, which connotes something less than real, with the notion of *virtual* that can better express the nature of an unfinished reality, and he replaces the rigidity of strict identities with a *multiplicity* that better reflects differences in the unfolding of reality. Not to be missed is the way that such terms help re-translate Nishida. Using *virtual* to translate *senzai-teki* (潜在的), for example, better expresses the priority of reality in the making than do terms like *latent* or *potential*.

I bring this foreword to an arbitrary close. By no means has it anticipated all the details of this innovative approach to Nishida. Two other English-language essays by Professor Higaki supplement the parallels he points out here: "Deleuze's Strange Affinity with the Kyoto School: Deleuze and Kitaro Nishida," in *Deleuze and Asia*, edited by Ronald Bogue, Hanping Chiu, Yu-lin Lee (Cambridge Scholars Publishing, 2014), 48–59; and "Japan as *Thousand Plateaus*," *Deleuze and Guattari Studies* 12:2 (2018). For now we may say that, to the extent that anyone can capture the *vital force* of Nishida's thought, Higaki's book goes a long way.

All citations of Nishida's works are from the *Complete Works of Nishida Kitarō*, New Edition, 24 vols., edited by Atsushi Takeda, Klaus Riesenhuber, Kunitsugu Kosaka, and Masakatsu Fujita (hereafter, *NKZ*). The citations will give the volume number followed by page number. Translator's notes are inserted within square brackets.

PREFACE TO *GAKUJUTSU BUNKO* EDITION

Ever since I was a college student in the 1980s, I wanted to attain a more flexible, broader understanding of the philosophy of the Kyoto School. Back then I thought of this as my own conceited desire regarding what appeared to me as a quite mysterious string of characters; but thinking of it now, various undercurrents were involved in that desire. That much has become clear to me in retrospect.

One of the professors under whom I studied at the time was Sakabe Megumi. In the 70s and 80s, when postmodernism was in vogue in Japan, Sakabe had initiated his project of reconceiving the potentiality of Japanese thought, such as that of Kuki Shūzō and Watsuji Tetsurō, from the standpoint of a Japanese thinker embarking on his own original meditations, with Nishida of the Kyoto School as his source of inspiration. This project was done in parallel with his work of reconceiving the history of thought within the larger context of Western philosophy—a work that centered on the study of Kant. Around the same time, Nakamura Yujirō published a work on Nishida Kitarō that attempted to re-interpret Nishida's discussion of acting intuition along the lines of contemporary theories of the body and creativity. Furthermore, a generation before the work of Sakabe and Nakamura, the psychiatrist Kimura Bin had been developing original ideas on psychopathology under the strong influence of Nishida's ideas.

These thinkers were affiliated neither with Nishida's direct students, nor with any lineage of students of those students. Yet they interpreted the philosophy of Nishida and the Kyoto School within the context of the contemporary philosophy of the time, and they were salient figures in this respect. Back then, their work had a great significance for the reading of Nishida and related thinkers.

Whether it be Nishida or Kuki or Watsuji, the thinkers of pre-war Japan were sensitive to the contemporary trends of Western philosophy (this is something that will be particularly emphasized in this book), and at the same time they approached these Western ideas in their own way, as something pertaining to their own questions. The reason why later philosophers (professional philosophers at universities), up until the present, have gone back to textual exegesis and are no longer asking questions is something that we must think about (although we cannot reject textual exegesis wholesale); however, I will not go into this issue here. Once we go through this kind of philological refinement, the criticism inevitably arises that the way the thinkers of the Kyoto School directly dealt with questions was very slipshod (and in particular, there is the hindsight criticism that their political stance was naïve). These criticisms are to some extent true. However, the way they approached their questions is sufficient to evoke in us a sense of profundity.

It is commonly alleged that we can discern in the work of the Kyoto School thinkers the opposition between East and West and between both Buddhist and Christian elements. This is by no means false. However, what we find when we read Nishida's texts is a sense of trust in modern Western ideas and methods, a trust that is so unmitigated that it is mysterious. Considering their immaturity that was inevitable at the time, perhaps we can call this "curiosity." They rummaged through the concepts of pragmatism, philosophy of life, phenomenology, hermeneutics, and the Nietzschean return to antiquity as if they were dealing with a "toy box" of ideas, and they seem to have experimentally applied Japanese terminology to these concepts. Yet, it cannot be denied that what they did inadvertently overlaps somewhat with the deconstructionist explorations of postmodernism.

The works of the Kyoto School are thus in some respect carefree, and exhibit some parallels with the irresponsibleness of postmodern philosophy. But at the same time, it must be acknowledged that, in these works, the authors are engaged in the *practice of creating various concepts*. In light of this circumstance, we can see that there is sufficient reason and significance in the fact that Sakabe, Nakamura, and Kimura, writing in the 70s and 80s, did not present their study of the philosophy of the Kyoto School as a study of Japanese thought, or as a "comparative study" of Japanese and Western thought in which the Japanese elements are fixed in an essentialist manner, but instead went far beyond this, deciphering their work with an eye towards the fecundity that results when heterogeneous elements meet.

The fact is that the questions that the thinkers of the Kyoto School were grappling with are colossal questions. In the case of Nishida, the themes of place and nothingness, acting intuition and *poiesis* are connected with the fundamental questions of contemporary theories of the body, action, and life. The theme of time and contingency that Kuki grasped, Watsuji's theory of persons based on the notion of "betweenness," and Watsuji's reflections on climate and culture present many stimulating issues in contemporary contexts, where temporality and environment are repeatedly made the subject of dispute. Furthermore, as shown by Kobayashi Toshiaki in his excellent book *Nishida Kitarō: Thinking the Foreign*,[1] the meditations that Nishida carried out in *Japanese* in particular make us think about the possibilities of *Japanese philosophy* and the fundamental issues surrounding the translation of thought; this is a point that I will touch upon in the main text of this book. To repeat, this is not something that can be understood within the ready-made framework of East and West. Rather, it is something that can only be understood as reaching a global universality.

It would be a shame if these texts of Nishida were to be ignored as mere relics of the past. But what kind of contrivance should we read into these texts? Although it may seem strange to those who know the subtitle of the original *Gendai Shinsho* edition of this book, I have attempted a kind of head-on approach.[2] That is, I have tried situating Nishida's texts within the context of Nishida's own age (this constitutes the Bergson connection), while at the same time highlighting the surplus that spills over this context (this constitutes the Deleuze connection).

---

1   Kobayashi Toshiaki, *Nishida Kitarō: Tasei no Buntai* (Tokyo: Ōta Shuppan, 1997). [While the subtitle literally translates as "the Style of Otherness," Kobayashi renders it in German as *Denken des Fremden.* I follow the German rendering here.]

2   [The subtitle of the original edition of this book, published in 2005, was "Deleuze, Bergson to Hibikiau Shiko" (Thought that Resonates with Deleuze and Bergson)]

Let us return to the connection with the postmodern context. Leaving aside the question of how we ought to evaluate it, postmodernism deals with a struggle to distance itself from the ideas of the period of modernity, while at the same time wholly accepting those ideas (in this sense a postmodernist is a modernist through and through). To interpret the fountainhead of Japanese philosophy in connection with postmodernism as Sakabe, Nakamura, and Kimura did is clearly a valid enterprise, for the early Japanese philosophers and postmodernists both share the same directionality, in that they both aspire to be modernists while at the same time must distance themselves from modernity. But today, twenty to thirty years after Sakabe and Nakamura, we also ought to keep in mind the following two points.

The first is that postmodernism has already become part of the history of thought. Not only Deleuze, whom I will be highlighting in this book, but also thinkers such as Foucault and Derrida, who were once celebrated as the forefront of fashion, have all passed away. Furthermore, their thought has already taken root in posterity and is being rewritten in different ways. At the same time, there have been intense discussions over where the origins of their thought lay, and whether their thought was a presentation of a remarkably deep intellectual-historical dynamism. In the case of Deleuze, it need hardly be said that the Bergson connection is extremely important, but so are the connections with the minor philosophies of the nineteenth century (Tarde, Peirce, differential philosophy).

As I will be emphasizing in this book, the thought of Nishida and the Kyoto School also has strong connections with pragmatism, philosophy of life, differential philosophy, and Nietzscheanism, and tries to create new concepts from these trends. In this sense, Nishida and the Kyoto School can be read as the *background of an already-classic postmodern philosophy*. Of course, the Kyoto School and postmodernism have no direct connections. But that is beside the point. What is significant is that the thinkers of the Kyoto School were thinking in the direction of postmodernism *avant la lettre*.

The second point that should be kept in mind is that *discussions of life* have gained a significance that they did not have in the past. This, of course, must be due to the transition in our knowledge and technologies pertaining to the immune system and genomes that took place in the 80s, and also the brain, which has been the subject of attention particularly in this century. In any case, in order to grasp the idea of life, we should first look back at the various trends of thought pertaining to life.

Nishida's thought starts from a philosophy of life, and from there goes on to discuss an environmental-theoretic theme called the logic of place (this is related to Watsuji's theory of climate and culture, which can be read as a prototype of the theory of affordance, that is to say, a kind of ecological philosophy), and the *poiesis* (creation/becoming) by the body and its acts (Kuki's philosophy of contingency is also none other than a theory of the instant and of becoming). It is easy to see that here we have an enumeration of topics that cannot be avoided in a discussion of life: life, place and environment, body, and creation. Albeit in very rough form, we have here the basic framework for a discussion of questions pertaining to life that have been made the central themes of postmodern philosophy, but have yet to be solved: difference and differenciation as differential,[3] the issue of biological individuals, and the contradictory identity of the individual and community. In this book, I have tried to present the *future* of Nishida's philosophy by exploring these questions. Nishida's philosophy can be understood not only as a *companion* of contemporary thought, but also as constituting its basis and, therefore, as containing elements that will lead it forward.

Yet there are many unresolved issues. Because I have laid great emphasis on the modernist and postmodernist aspects of Nishida in this book, I have not been able to go into discussions of the Kyoto School within the context of Japanese culture or theories of Japan

---

3　[Throughout this book, the author makes a distinction between *saika* (差異化) and *bunka* (分化), which both translate into English as "differentiation." According to the author, the former refers to the differentiation of a virtual realm while the latter refers to the differentiation that takes place in an already actualized, individualized realm (as when we speak of cellular differentiation). Taking advantage of the distinction between *différentiation* and *différenciation* in French, throughout this book "differentiation" will be used to render *saika*, and the neologism "differenciation" (with a "c") to render *bunka*. The author also makes frequent use of the term *bibun* (微分), which refers to differentiation in the mathematical sense. To avoid confusion with the former two senses, this will be rendered as either "differential" or "mathematical differentiation."]

(which should be done in view of postcolonial or political critiques of the Kyoto School). The short essay on Taisho vitalism that has been included as a supplementary chapter of this book expresses one possible approach, but since it deals with the relation between the Kyoto School and French philosophy, it is inadequate in this respect. For instance, connections should be drawn at some point with the discussions of the Japanese psyche from antiquity, pioneered by Orikuchi Shinobu, Yanagita Kunio, and Watsuji. Furthermore, an examination of the Kyoto School's religious aspects (religion itself being a bodily practice), namely, the connection with Zen Buddhism (a form of Buddhism particularly indigenized to Japan) cannot be omitted.

Insofar as this century is a postcolonial one, it is our task to reflect philosophically upon Japan from the standpoint of the diversity of world cultures, and upon Japan's peculiar place (from the outset) as a crossroad of civilizations. My hope is that through such diverse studies, the potentiality of the texts of the Kyoto School, one of the beginnings of philosophy in Japan, *will be realized at a time and place unbeknownst to the writers.* And this is precisely what will demonstrate the fundamental force of philosophy.

INTRODUCTION
WHO IS NISHIDA KITARŌ?

The Appeal of Nishida's Philosophy

Nishida Kitarō possesses all the elements that a philosopher must possess in order to be attractive: a bizarre style of writing that does not admit of easy comprehension, the repetitive overuse of a peculiar jargon and phrases that show no consideration for the reader, the wild enthusiasm of the people around him which today may even seem abnormal, and the excessive anticipation and exultation of Japan's first original philosophizing, something much more than a mere importation or reception of novel foreign ideas.

To continue the list, there is the shower of both praise and criticism that Nishida was subject to in connection with his being part of a distinct school of thought, the Kyoto School, and his consequent isolation and loneliness. There are the many contradictory statements regarding Nishida within the political context of the Second World War: on the one hand, he is defended as a progressive critic of the fascist regime, while on the other he is despised as a supporter of the Greater East Asia Co-Prosperity Sphere that represents the Oriental standpoint of thought. The position of Kyoto as opposed to Tokyo may also be a subtle factor here. There is the traditional background of the modern city of Kyoto, and an accompanying sense of orthodoxy that may become exclusionary, a sense that is aggravated by Kyoto's position as a minor city compared to Tokyo.

But above all else, there is the constant rewriting of one's thoughts, the complete modification of one's positions. Nonetheless, there is the tenacity of repeating over and over the same theme, so much so that the reader is left dumbfounded. And yet there is the torrent-like intelligence with which Nishida expands his thought into diverse territories as his interests dictate, an intelligence that is even de-territorial, that is, ranges over all disciplines. There is the staggering amount of texts, particularly after Nishida's retirement from Kyoto Imperial University, when he is entering his elder years. And even there, there is the thirst-like thought that keeps probing into the same issues, all the while changing positions many times.

While the "bizarre" character of Nishida's writing style has been highlighted by Kobayashi Toshiaki's critique,[1] Nishida's lectures were also of a nature that can be easily imagined. He would constantly repeat himself, trying to craft new expressions each time. To some people, this would have appeared as the very birth of a philosophy. It would have seemed as if Nishida were embracing philosophy, itself a product of Western civilization, with his own body and presenting its genesis in a radical manner.

But at the same time, others saw Nishida's lectures as an irresponsible rambling, lacking in considerations of the history of philosophy and in systematic orderliness. Tanaka Michitarō, who became Professor of History of Philosophy at Kyoto University after the war, remarked in a dialogue with Ueyama Shunpei about Nishida: "he's just babbling whatever comes to his mind, without having studied the matter."[2] It cannot be denied that there is some truth in this remark, a truth about the other side of the enthusiasm emanated by Nishida's adherents. Whether one sees in Nishida a genuine, steel-like originality of thought, or a frivolous string of words expressing whatever comes to mind without any orthodox textual research, it can be said that these two aspects are really two sides of the same coin.

On the one hand, Nishida is praised for his originality of thought, his acquiring of enthusiastic readers and disciples, and his establishment of a serious Japanese philosophy; and on the other, his work is met with sentimental resistance and criticized for its unintelligibility, even being described as the typical kind of cryptic bad writing. Furthermore, there is the emotional reaction against the anti-regime authority of the Kyoto School (a group of people who were emotionally close because of their anti-regime stance), and there is Nishida's

---

1   Kobayashi, *op. cit.*

2   Atsushi Takeda, *Monogatari "Kyōto Gakuha"* (Tokyo: Chūō Kōron Shinsha, 2001). The original dialogue with Shunpei Ueyama was published as an Appendix to *Nihon no Meicho 47: Nishida Kitarō* (Tokyo: Chūō Kōron Shinsha, 1970).

lonely life and large amount of texts, the reverse side of the enthusiasm with which he was received. Perhaps the imbalance of these elements was something necessary in order for philosophy to be philosophy, in order to begin addressing the words to which only the description "Japanese philosophy" can be appended—a description that was from the outset (and will always be) a *contradictio in adjecto.* (And perhaps this situation has not changed even in our postmodern age). I believe that it is necessary for us to retrace this imbalance of Nishida in a positive manner. For this imbalance is, paradoxically, connected to something that makes the ambition of philosophy appealing—the ambition to completely narrate this world and its genesis (and this is by no means restricted to the situation in Japan).

What I want to illustrate in this book is the appeal of Nishida's philosophy as indicated by this imbalance. This is because Nishida's texts display what I consider to be real philosophy, philosophy that ought to be sketched. There is really no other reason why one should read or write about a philosophical text.

Furthermore, I think that Nishida's appeal is due in large part to the fact that he probed "life" to the bottom and modeled his own thought on it, because to think "life" directly is to grasp emerging existence directly and try to logicize it through and through: it is this sincere attempt to completely describe becoming—something that is incredibly difficult to capture in words—from various angles that, in part, constitutes the inevitable and decisive imbalance of Nishida's philosophy. Furthermore, Nishida's philosophy of life offers us many suggestions today, when fundamental ideas concerning "life" and "becoming" are sought.

The Man Nishida Kitarō

We are getting ahead of ourselves. Who is Nishida Kitarō? Let us take a glance at what Nishida did, insofar as it is necessary for our purposes. For the imbalance and appeal of Nishida that I illustrated previously can be explained in large part by the age and environment in which he lived.

Nishida Kitarō was born in 1870 and died in 1945. He was born in Unoke in Ishikawa Prefecture. He studied at the Fourth High School (under the old system) of Kanazawa, and then enrolled at Tokyo Imperial University as an elective student. After graduation, he taught at rural high schools, moving from one workplace to another, until he eventually settled at Kyoto Imperial University. In the later period of his life, he moved back and forth between Kyoto and Kamakura, spending almost all of his time thinking. The originality of his lectures had always caught attention since he was young, but later in his life his writing activities became more and more vigorous in an essential sense.

An Inquiry into the Good (1911), an early work of Nishida that is based on his high school lectures and is only the prologue of his entire life of thinking, has gained more readers than he could have ever imagined. There is a legend that people waited in lines to buy the first volume of his collected works before its release, published by Iwanami Shoten after the war, soon after Nishida's death. It is not the case that Nishida's philosophy was properly understood, or that the Japanese people back then were intellectually superior to the Japanese people today. But I think we ought to pay attention to the fact that Nishida was a philosopher who was *read*. It cannot be denied that Nishida's words functioned as a sort of salvation during that age.

Furthermore, this phenomenon is not restricted to Nishida's age. In contrast to Nishida's own lamentation—a lamentation that is so stubborn that it is almost neurotic—that his logic "has not yet received any attention,"[3] it is clear from the works that have been published in the last ten or twenty years that interest in his philosophy has not waned (although it is probably true that Nishida's remark that his logic "has not received any attention" is an expression of a truth). Rather, it can even be said that, with the disappearance of the sterile opposition that existed for some time between left wing critics who attacked Nishida's political attitude on the one hand and the stubborn defenders of Nishida on the other, the trend that has become prominent today is to approach Nishida's texts in a straightforward manner.

---

3   *NKZ*, 10: 431.

Whether one approaches Nishida's philosophy from the stand-point of East/West cultural comparison or from a historical stand-point (an approach that I do not take), or as a fundamental philo-sophical text with a view towards an application to today's problems (the approach that I do take), Nishida's philosophy continues to possess a force that attracts many people from different perspectives. (The interpretation of Nishida has been, in some sense, like a bench-mark for Japanese philosophers, by which one can see the thrust of their thinking. Here, I will list the major works on Nishida that have appeared since the 80s:

- Nakamura Yujirō, *Nishida Kitarō*, 2 Vols. (Tokyo: Iwanami, 2001)
- Ueda Shizuteru, *Nishida Kitarō wo yomu* (Reading Nishida Kitarō) (Tokyo: Iwanami, 1991); *Nishida Kitarō: Ningen no Shōgai toiukoto* (Nishida Kitarō: The Life of Man) (Tokyo: Iwanami, 1995); *Nishida Tetsugaku eno Michibiki: Keiken to Jikaku* (Introduction to Nishida's Philosophy: Experience and Self-Awareness) (Tokyo: Iwanami, 1998)
- Nitta Yoshihiro, *Gendai no Toi toshiteno Nishida Tetsugaku* (Nishida's Phi-losophy as a Contemporary Question) (Tokyo: Iwanami, 1998)
- Ōhashi Ryōsuke, *Nishida Tetsugaku no Sekai: Aruiwa Tetsugaku no Ten-kai* (The World of Nishida's Philosophy: Or, the Revolution of Philosophy) (Tokyo; Chikuma Shobō, 1995)
- Fujita Masakatsu, *Gendai Shisō toshiteno Nishida Kitarō* (Nishida Kitarō as Contemporary Thought) (Tokyo: Kōdansha, 1998)
- Nakaoka Narifumi, *Watashi to Deau tame no Nishida Kitarō* (Nishida Kitarō in Order to Meet Myself) (Tokyo: Demadosha, 1999)
- Kosaka Kunitsugu, *Nishida Kitarō no Shisō* (The Thought of Nishida Kitarō) (Tokyo: Kōdansha, 2002)

Again, Nishida's intellectual activities in Kyoto have had an influ-ence that goes beyond his own thought and domain, shaping the direction of an entire age. His influence ranges over many original philosophers such as Tanabe Hajime, Watusji Tetsurō, Miki Kiyoshi, Kuki Shūzō, and Tosaka Jun, comprising both right- and left-wing thinkers. These thinkers are not, of course, disciples of Nishida in the straightforward sense of the word; some of them have little intel-lectual connection to Nishida, while others have heavily criticized Nishida and left him. But by any standard, there has not been a period in Japan when academic philosophy was developed in as dazzling a manner as this age. And one cannot deny that it is Nishida who sits symbolically at the center of this age. Among the thinkers of this age, it was Nishida himself who most purely and directly attempted to develop a philosophy. Certainly, it was this thirst for philosophy that created the energy of Kyoto in diverse ways, including politics.

The topics that Nishida addressed are diverse. The slogan of his early period was "pure experience" (*An Inquiry into the Good*). The system of pure experience was then re-conceptualized as "self-awareness" (*Intuition and Reflection in Self-Awareness*). Nishida then shifted to a philosophy of "place," where the issue of "expression" comes to the fore (*From the Acting to the Seeing*). After this period, Nishida began emphasizing "absolute nothingness," which can be interpreted as a religious state of experience (*The Self-Aware System of the Universal*); this gave rise to criticism regarding the scholarliness of Nishida's work (the criticism of Tanabe Hajime, once Nishida's assistant professor, is important in highlighting the significance of Nishida's thought). In response to this criticism, Nishida went on to modify his conception of nothingness (*The Self-Aware Determination of Nothingness*).

The key concepts that give Nishida's later thought its distinct color are "acting intuition" and the "absolute contradictory self-identity." During this period, the titles of Nishida's published works become unified as "Philosophical Essays Vol. X" and are not noteworthy. He gradually approaches what could be called the final form of a philosopher. He continues to produce, one by one, fragmentary texts wherein ideas are developed endlessly.

It is impossible to explain in just a few words what Nishida discusses in these texts. He develops original interpretations of many European philosophers such as Bergson, the Neo-Kantians, Fichte, Aristotle, Leibniz, and, of course, Descartes, Kant, and Hegel. But he was never a mere exponent or expositor of *someone else's* philosophy.

The themes that Nishida discussed are also diverse. From his early theory of pure experience, through to his idea of absolute nothingness, which is often connected with the experience of Zen Buddhism, and toward the end of his life, there is a strong element of religious metaphysics in Nishida's thought. But when one approaches Nishida's texts from this standpoint, one is surprised to find an interest in set theory and the foundations of mathematics, consistent from the beginning to the end of his life, and a powerful will to logicize. His thought also displays its sharpness in genres as diverse as history and art. Even with respect to *what* it is that Nishida discussed, it is difficult to attain consensus.

Many things can be said about Nishida's appeal and the character of his thought from what has already been discussed. But at this point, we cannot omit an explanation of the age and place in which Nishida lived, in order to consider the character of Nishida's thought. In particular, I want to focus on the following three points.

The Age of Nishida

The first is the peculiarity of the *age* in which Nishida wrote his philosophical works. Not much reflection is necessary in order to realize that this was an age of radical transition. The European sciences were flooding Japan at an exhilarating pace, and a modern university system had just been established. The elite intelligentsia had to import new ideas and institutions without a moment's rest; otherwise Japan would be left behind. The people were inexorably incorporated into the country's imperialist strategy. It was an age of industrialization and urbanization. The educational and academic systems were vastly changing. Such was the age in which Nishida was situated.

In the case of fields such as medicine or technology, where the results are clearly visible, perhaps the wise choice would have been to study abroad, import these sciences, and present one's own visible results. Indeed, many pre-war scholars in Japan took this route. But in the case of literature or philosophy, where an original relation between one's words and situation is demanded from the outset, complications are inevitable. The importation of European sciences into Japan, the issue of translating these sciences, and the vexation of the intelligentsia after the Meiji era all complicated the situation. A natural consequence of this is the emergence of a tendency to glorify Europe on the one hand, and of an Oriental stance on the other. We can see this kind of stereotypical dualism seeping into Nishida's philosophical milieu.

It has been common practice to project the spirit of this age onto Nishida's own footsteps. This can be seen in the sheer number of biographies and cultural accounts that have been written on Nishida, including his high school years. Nishida's life can be depicted as a kind of *Bildungsroman* peculiar to a young man of the Meiji era. His philosophical pilgrimage consists of various forms of resistance, failures, and suffering, and it culminates in an outlook of high originality. One may regard Nishida's life and experiences as typical of a man who lives amid the encounter of different civilizations and in an age of transition.

A topic that is often taken up is Nishida's affinity, both practical and theoretical, with Zen Buddhism. The fact that Nishida practiced Zen meditation as a young man, and that the eminent D. T. Suzuki was a friend of Nishida, are important factors here. Another factor that supports the reading of Nishida as the place of the encounter of two civilizations is the fact that he himself emphasized at one point in his life the contrast between the Occidental culture of "form" and the Oriental culture of the "form of the formless."

Although it involves stereotypical dichotomies, one cannot outright reject the claim that there is an imbalance in Nishida, an imbalance that stems from the circumstance that he had no choice but to think amid boundaries: the boundary between the feudal age and the modern age of science and technology, and the boundary between the Occidental and Oriental.

However, I believe that this kind of cultural, historical understanding of Nishida has the danger of failing to capture the appeal that the erratic nature of Nishida's texts possess—not to deny the possibility that cultural studies and postcolonial studies may shed light on various aspects of the encounter of civilizations and the translation of thought. To be marginal is, in fact, nothing special. For in reality, every one of us is already marginal. But it is also true that Nishida had no choice but to live a marginal life with vigor, in a peculiar sense.

The Place of Nishida

The second point that we ought to consider is the *place* where Nishida lived, namely, Kyoto—in contrast to Tokyo. Regardless of how Nishida himself thought or willed, the image of Nishida is very strongly linked with that of Kyoto.

Many biographies of Nishida mention the fact that he was not an official student of Tokyo Imperial University. From the outset, he was excluded from the orthodox academic system (the student production system). He taught at high schools in Kanazawa and Yamaguchi, moving from one place to another, until he was nearly forty. He suffered various hardships during this period. And suddenly he was appointed professor of Kyoto Imperial University.

Roughly, the standard illustration continues as follows: Tokyo is practical and bureaucratic, doing nothing but half-blindly imitating the West and following the state's *fukoku-kyōhei* policy [policy for increasing national prosperity and military strength]. Kyoto, on the other hand, is open-minded and fertile with academic creativity. It is a counterforce, open to developing its own thought, precisely because it is minor and excluded. Intricately bound up with this is the background of Kyoto's tradition from medieval age.

It is probably true that Kyoto Imperial University embodied the ideal of being the antithesis of Tokyo Imperial University, both on its own initiative and through the appraisal of others, and that it fulfilled this function with astuteness. Certainly, there is a kind of ethos that is possible precisely because one is not at the center. In order for scholarship to be original, this kind of ethos must always be thoroughgoing. It cannot be denied that the Kyoto School, of which Nishida was the core, was able to become an original academic institution precisely because it scraped together people who could be called the "residue" of Tokyo.

This kind of depiction—a depiction that emphasizes the minor aspect of Nishida—resonates in a subtle way with Nishida's own personal circumstances. It is certain that Nishida attained his own thought after going through various hardships. It is true that his comparatively wealthy family was facing a downfall, that he suffered persecution due to his opposition to the militarist tendencies of the age, and that he went through various personal hardships, including the death of his first wife and four of his eight children. These circumstances fit in all too easily with the image of Nishida as an excluded man, filled with resentment. Many biographies of Nishida emphasize this dark aspect and thereby illustrate his life in vivid contrasts.

It might be argued that this kind of image of Nishida as a minority serves, in one respect, to incite a peculiar idolization of the man. Yet

I do not think that the air of power that surrounds the entire man Nishida—an air due to his being marginalized—should be neglected. As I have indicated, the imbalance that runs through Nishida's thought consists in the fact that he is always focused on one thing, and at the same time traverses a broad range of fields. That is, in handling one problem, Nishida pulls various domains into his discourse, immediately and forcefully. For example, one gets the impression that Nishida is discussing Zen Buddhism, mathematics, issues of the body, and political issues all on the same plane. Some may call this "freedom of thought"; others may see in it the questionable trait that often accompanies this form of de-territorial knowledge, namely, *frivolity* of manner. In the political context, for instance, Nishida's attitude certainly does give rise to naïve precariousness. His interpretation of the Japanese imperial family in terms of his notion of the "absolute contradictory self-identity" is a typical example; see *The Problem of Japanese Culture*.

However, it cannot be denied that Nishida's tenacity of thinking through the same problem in a hybrid manner, without resting his feet in one particular place, is a productive reflection of the minor nature of the "place" in which he was situated, namely, Kyoto as opposed to Tokyo.

Yet is not this kind of marginality in fact something that anyone could become? Should not this marginality be a state into which anyone ought to drive oneself when developing ideas in a productive manner, regardless of where they are or what kind of position they are in? Thus, we should not turn this marginality into a concrete object like Kyoto. It is clear what kind of path waits when we seek marginality in a concrete object. If the privileged position of Kyoto were to link with the reactionary force of a sense of orthodoxy—a sense due to its being excluded—then it would be deprived of its lightness and de-territorial nature. If the anti-regime authority loses its view of itself as a contradictory movement, then it risks the danger of becoming the most powerful reaction. There are various opinions as to the nature of Kyoto after Nishida was transformed into the legendary "regime." One should understand the relation between Nishida and Kyoto with a clear view of these merits and demerits, that is, Nishida's power of assimilation and power of evoking reaction.

In the Transition of Thought

We have seen the imbalance of Nishida's thought and its consequent appeal in the context of the peculiarity of the period of Japan
in which he lived, as well as Nishida's own hardship-filled self-for-
mation, and the place in which he was active, namely, Kyoto. These
are themes that cannot be avoided in any discussion of Nishida.
But thirdly, we must not omit the other factor that constitutes the
thoroughness and hybridity of Nishida's philosophy. This is something that can be called the "global simultaneity" of his thought. The
period into which Nishida was born possesses a great significance for
the transition of thought at the global level.

Freud, the founder of psychoanalysis; Saussure, who conceived
semiology; Husserl, the founder of phenomenology, a school of
thought that will play a decisive role in the twentieth century; and
Bergson, who directly influenced Nishida and gave rise to one of the
trends of the philosophy of life, were all contemporaries of Nishida
in the sense that they were all born in the latter half of the nineteenth
century, although they come from different places (if we were to
adopt a broader time frame, then we may also include William James,
the American pragmatist, and Ernst Mach, who was active in Vienna).

The trajectory of thought that these thinkers depicted without rest
at the beginning of the twentieth century, after many twists and turns,
has become the direct source of the thought of the twenty-first century.
Even today, after having gone through structuralism and postmodernism, it is becoming ever more difficult to think the constitution of our
world without utilizing the tools provided by trends of thought such as
the philosophy of life, phenomenology, semiology, and psychoanalysis.
It is certainly among these thinkers that Nishida's texts ought to be situated.

In a sense it is natural that this was an age of new ideas. Modern philosophy itself had become trapped in a *cul-de-sac* in Hegel. The universal age as well had probably foreseen the dark destination toward which
the progress and glory of modernity was heading. Notwithstanding the
rapid development of science and technology, a typical feeling of danger was sprouting at the turn of the century—a feeling that, in the near

future, this rapid development would give rise to a surplus or monster that would not fit into the progressive ideals of modernity.

The trends of thought during this age, therefore, strove toward *thoroughness*. They sought impulsively to approach the world, not as something that could be enmeshed in a dubious, bloated system, but as something immediate, simple, and raw—something that appears to us as real. To put it simply, this was an impulse to grasp life, experience, and phenomena *purely*. The key to capturing the new age consisted in how close one could approach *purity*.

Of course, there are many possible views about what is *pure*. The philosophers of Vienna, with Mach at their center, discussed the purity of sense data, and this was later transformed into a radical purity in the direction of logic and language (the early Wittgenstein arose from this context). And it need hardly be said that the reduction to pure consciousness taken up by Husserl, who in some respects is an heir of the Vienna tradition, is possessed by the impulse towards purity, to undermine the assumptions of the natural attitude of modern thought, return to the facts themselves in a thorough manner, and redo everything from scratch.

And then there are Bergson and James. Both of these thinkers presented the notions of pure duration or pure experience and aimed at a description of the world as it is, prior to the separation of the subject and object (the "I" and the object). In this sense, they are directly linked with the early Nishida, whose theme was also pure experience. In any case, it is clear that the thought of this period sought for a pure description of the world in a radical way. It was an age where people were filled with the enthusiasm to completely destroy the machinery of modernity and give rise to something new. Nishida's thought was intimately bound up with this movement of the age.

The endeavor to redo philosophy purely from scratch is not something that can be pursued in a single-minded fashion. The impulse toward purity is forced to seriously doubt or reflect upon the purity of whatever it discerns. The desire to completely describe the world in terms of the purity of language or signs will eventually arrive at the recognition that language itself is vague. The explication of pure consciousness will immediately run against the dark basis that supports consciousness, such as the *Lebenswelt* that Husserl discerned. This is a situation that prompts that Derridean notion that the very idea of a pure consciousness is impossible.

Bergson's idea of pure duration also faces a fundamental doubt. While Bergson exerted a significant influence on the next generation thinker Merleau-Ponty, and, later still, on Deleuze, one can point out the difficulties involved in thoroughly investigating, within Bergson's framework, the purity that Bergson describes in a rather naïve way.

We should, however, keep in mind the following point: the attempt to return to something pure and describe the world from scratch will, at some point, have to confront the naiveté and untenability of its assumptions. Yet the thought of the twentieth century (including semiology and psychoanalysis) certainly has its origins in this attitude of dismantling the machinery of modernity and closing in on the real in a plain and simple fashion. Although the endeavor may be criticized from within, the splendor of twentieth century thought would have been impossible without this impulse towards purity.

The Global Simultaneity of Nishida

What is even more important is the place of Nishida within this context. Nishida's radical striving for pure experience concurs, via James and Bergson, with the global movement towards purity. Yet Nishida's struggle and changes of attitude—which happen, to such extent, that they may even seem abnormal—can be said to show that the attempt of the theory of pure experience to grasp the real world as it is cannot be sustained by itself, and that it is confronted by many problems from within. Faced with his philosophy's self-implosion, Nishida had to think through the consequences of purity by himself, without losing sight of the impulsive part of philosophy.

Nishida's thought, which takes its point of departure via the concept of pure experience, goes well beyond the context of modern Japanese philosophy. It is from the outset related to the global simultaneity of thought, which claims that we must return to the real given in immediacy. Furthermore, Nishida thoroughly investigated the problems involved in the notion of pure experience. Therefore, there is nothing peculiar in discussing the resonance between Nishida and the contemporary and postmodern thought of the latter half of the twentieth century. While there are many directions in contemporary philosophy, insofar as it passes through the project of radical purification and is presented as a critical reassessment of the foundations of such an enterprise, the ideas that Nishida worked out independently can be said to overlap with these developments. I believe that this is a crucial point when reading Nishida today.

What I should emphasize at this point is that, in what follows, I will deliberately superimpose the progression of Nishida's thought with the development of the philosophy of life that flows from Bergson to Deleuze, the critical successor of Bergson. I will utilize Bergson and Deleuze rather tenaciously, as co-runners, so to speak, to help interpret Nishida's thought. I want to make clear that the reason I take such an approach is not because I want to discuss the proximity of Oriental and postmodern thought, a stereotypical theme. Rather, it is because I want to highlight the fact that Nishida, in his global simultaneity, pursued the consequences of the philosophy of purification to its ultimate form.

Finally, mention should be made of Nishida's acute sense of his age, a sense that can even be characterized as de-territorial. It displays the healthy function of the intellect particularly in relation to topics of natural science, such as set theory, the foundations of mathematics, and the life sciences. In Nishida, we can feel in a deep way the same kind of thought as that of Bergson and Deleuze, in the sense that he linked his philosophy with the natural sciences and thereby derived ideas about life and becoming.

However, at this stage, it is sufficient to point out that the hybridity of Nishida's thought reaches into the extreme radicality of global simultaneity, encompassing all the consequences of purification.

Nishida's Philosophy of Life

So far, we have discussed the peripheral aspects of Nishida. Now let us ask again: what is Nishida's philosophy? I believe that Nishida is a philosopher who discussed life. His philosophy is brilliant precisely because of the thorough way in which he discussed life.

However, it is not very common to describe Nishida's philosophy as a "philosophy of life." There are many keywords pertaining
to Nishida: pure experience, self-awareness, place, absolute nothingness, acting intuition, and the absolute contradictory self-identity.
It is by all means possible to examine Nishida's philosophy from the
standpoint of these keywords, each of which represents a stage of
Nishida's thought. The philosophy of self-awareness, the philosophy
of place, and the philosophy of nothingness are directions that have
been favored by Nishida scholars. The philosophy of history and the
theory of science and technology are also perspectives that are often
adopted recently. Furthermore, since Nishida frequently deals with
other philosophers, another approach is to treat Nishida as a developer of the thought of those philosophers. For instance, Nishida can
be portrayed as the developer of James's and Bergson's concepts of
pure experience and "pure duration," of the Fichtean notion of "awareness," or of the Hegelian "dialectic." Or he can be portrayed as the
Japanese Heidegger, with the philosophy of place and nothingness
at his center. It would not be very productive to discuss what is right
and what is wrong with such approaches. Of course, each approach
has its own persuasiveness and appeal. Moreover, it is the strength of
Nishida's text that it induces these somewhat conflicting ideas.

Yet I want to take a single, definite approach. I understand from
the outset that it can only be a one-sided approach (but is it possible to approach a philosopher like Nishida in a way that is not one-
sided?); namely, as I have already stated, I want to approach Nishida
as the developer of a "philosophy of life." More specifically, I want to
approach Nishida as someone who discussed life, and who resonates
at a deep level with Bergson, who developed at the beginning of the
twentieth century a philosophy of life, and with Deleuze, who critically adopted the ideas of Bergson and established one of the foundations of postmodern philosophy. To repeat, it is not my intention
to conduct a comparative study of these thinkers, presenting various
evidences to show that they resemble each other. Nor is it my intention to extol Nishida by arguing that the range of his thought reaches
postmodernism. That is not what I want to do. What I want to argue
is that Nishida, at his core, is a philosopher of life.

Here I would like to explain Bergson and Deleuze a bit, including their connections with Nishida. Bergson (1859–1941) was a French philosopher who lived roughly during the same time as Nishida. His works include *Time and Liberty* (1889), which discusses the relation between time and free will by taking up the notion of "pure duration," depicted as a psychological quality; *Matter and Memory* (1896), which focuses on the mind-body problem and develops an original theory of "pure memory"; and *Creative Evolution* (1907), which examines life as *élan vital* (vital impetus) on the basis of the results of evolutionary theory at the time. In these works, Bergson consistently attempted to explicate the nature of life, which exists only in flux, at an ontological level.

Nishida's early concept of pure experience is closely related in content to Bergson's pure duration. As I will explain in detail later, Nishida and Bergson have a strong affinity, in that they both developed a theory of life and discussed "organic relations." Furthermore, Bergson's concept of pure memory, the culmination of his ideas on life, overlaps in large degree with Nishida's theory of place. At this stage, the two men can be said to be moving in the same direction, in the sense that both are seeking for the foundation upon which organic existence itself can be situated.

Deleuze (1925–95) was a French philosopher who was active in the latter half of the twentieth century. The ideas presented in his *Anti-Oedipus* (1972) and *A Thousand Plateaus* (1980) are often considered to be theories of postmodern culture and discussions of capitalism. Indeed, Deleuze's works are multi-faceted. However, as can be seen in his early work, *The Philosophy of Bergson* (1966), and his philosophical magnum opus, *Difference and Repetition* (1968), the core of his thought is his follow-up to Bergson's philosophy of life. Adopting from Bergson terms such as difference, virtuality, heterogeneity, multiplicity, and differenciation, Deleuze scrutinized the limits of Bergson's theory and rewrote it into a contemporary ontology of becoming.

This aspect of Deleuze, as a critical successor to the philosophy of life, indicates a critical link to Nishida's struggles during his middle and later years. The thought of the two men overlap in that they both attempted to grasp becoming as it is in itself as *poiesis*.[4] I believe that we can see the connection between the two men in the fact that they both follow each step of the arguments of the philosophy of life and present becoming as "autopoiesis," the culminating point of those steps. I want to depict Nishida's thought as a philosophy of life by taking up such connections with the tradition of the philosophy of life. But here, instead of rushing ahead, let us follow the developments of Nishida's thought.

The One Thing That Nishida Discussed

As I have already mentioned, a characteristic of Nishida's thought is that he discussed the same topic in various ways. Even when he takes up different themes, in principle, he tenaciously changes his approach to one problem. What, then, is the one problem that Nishida discussed?

To put it plainly, it is the problem of thinking the "I" that exists in this world from the perspective of practice. This issue and the question "what is the world in the making?" are two sides of the same coin. It is at the junction where the "acting I" and "world in the making" meet that Nishida discerns reality:

> It seems to me that philosophy has not even once thought truly from the standpoint of the acting self. Therefore, the question "what is this real world wherein I act?" has, at a fundamental level, been left unanswered.[5]

This is something like a declaration of war against traditional philosophy. While this statement is from Nishida's late period, the attitude expressed here is consistent with his attitude in his earliest works. To "practice," to "act," to "make" (*poieo*); to be the world that forms itself; to radically throw oneself into the world that acts and flows, and to not see the world apart from the standpoint of "action"—this is the foundational axis of Nishida's ideas. It is from this perspective that Nishida emerges as a theorist of life. In this context, he engages with questions

---

4   "*Poiesis*" is a word of Greek origin that Nishida uses to refer to the act of making and creating in action. In particular, it becomes a fundamental term in the later Nishida.

5   *NKZ*, 6: 135.

such as: what is this living "I"? What is this world in the making? These are the fundamental themes of any discussion of life.

From Pure Experience to Self-Awareness

The theme of the early Nishida is pure experience. This is a depiction of the world as it is immediately given. To borrow Nishida's expression, pure experience is the situation in which "it is not the case that there is first an individual and then experience; rather, there is first experience and then an individual."[6] It is not the case that a subject called the "I" (a self that is posited on this side of the world) exists from the outset, from which the object (assumed to exist on the other side of the world) can be described. Rather, the "I" is living a pure and undifferenciated experience in which the "I" and the "world" are indistinguishable. It is the error of modern epistemology to draw a distinction from the outset where there ought to be none. It is because of this distinction that the pseudo-problem "what is the relation between the I and world?" arises.

If one wants to seek the real, one must trek into the foundation of experience that is prior to the epistemological sundering. When I smell the scent of a rose, there is no distinction between myself and the scent. There must be such a pure foundation of experience; and it is the theory of pure experience that develops this idea. This state of pure experience is by no means a vague, mystic state. Nishida is only investigating pure experience as a setting of "action" in which the "I" and world are unified and connected.

Here, it will be helpful to consider the fact that Bergson depicts this kind of state as a flow of time called "pure duration" (while it is only after completing *An Inquiry into the Good* that Nishida seriously reads Bergson, the thoughts of the two men are linked in an extremely intimate way, as contemporaneous thoughts). It was in the context of motion that Bergson criticized the dualism of subject and object and presented the infinite linking of the two. To reject dualism and discern a pure state of affairs is an effort to grasp the becoming of

---

6   *NKZ*, 1: 6, 7.

the world as it is in itself, a world in which the I and world move while infinitely identifying themselves. Nishida also shares this context.

Next, Nishida depicts a philosophy of self-awareness. The immediate unity of the I and world that was emphasized as "practice" in the theory of pure experience is here replaced in an even stronger form, as self-awareness. Self-awareness is the "act" of "determining" oneself—a self that is unified with the world in act—in that act itself. The I that is identified with the world does not from the outset possess a centrality called the self. Rather, it must delineate the self within the movement that is infinitely identified with the world. It is through such delineation that both the self and the world can emerge. This "practice" of delineation is cast in terms of self-awareness. However, this determination within the infinite totality possesses aspects that are not simple. Here, Nishida, citing the words of the American philosopher Royce, likens the function of self-awareness to the act of drawing a map that depicts oneself. The act of drawing a map in which oneself is drawn involves a self-referential practice in which the drawer and the drawn object are constantly transformed, due to the reflexivity of drawing and being drawn. Nishida's theory of self-awareness is an attempt to grasp the world and self while disclosing this endless movement.

Place, Absolute Nothingness, and Practice

Nishida's theory of place has the tendency to emphasize space as opposed to the flow of time. Thus, it may seem that it loses touch with the practical. Furthermore, the fact that the theory of place is discussed in a work entitled *From the Acting to the Seeing* (1927) may reinforce this impression. There Nishida emphasizes the "intelligible" and ultimately reaches the theme of absolute nothingness. Ostensibly, it may seem that Nishida's argument for philosophy as practice has landed him in the nothingness of rest and contemplation, the foundation of practice. But that is not the case. While it is true that during this period, Nishida takes up what he calls the "form of the formless" and emphasizes it as Oriental as opposed to Occidental, his theory of place and of nothingness—the limit of place—does not preclude the theme of practice. This is understandable, given that Nishida's thought during this period moves toward the theme of "expression."

The notions of place and nothingness depict the end or limit that is demanded by the function of the infinite as act. However, while it discerns the ground called place and the limit of place that is nothingness, it attempts to explain how practice, as the expression of the determination of that ground, can take place.

In the later Nishida, the theme of "action" becomes even more vivid and perspicuous. The titles of his essays during this period— "The Standpoint of Acting Intuition," "Practice and Object Cognition," "Acting Intuition," "Introduction to Practical Philosophy," "Poiesis and Practice"—directly express the function of "*poiesis*."

The keywords during this period are *acting intuition* and the *absolute contradictory self-identity*. Both of these concepts have to do with the theme of action. Nishida's theory of acting intuition, which combines two words—*acting* and *intuition*—that from a certain standpoint may seem to be conflicting terms, can be interpreted as expressing a transition in Nishida's thought; namely, instead of *from the acting to the seeing*, he is now moving in a direction in which *acting* (practice) and *seeing* (intuition) are identified, that is, he is taking an even stronger position with respect to practice.

Then there is the absolute contradictory self-identity. This term is often taken up as the typical example of Nishida's obscure jargon. However, it is a term that embodies Nishida's desire to logicize in a simple way the situation of becoming, in which the self is constantly changing in practice, bearing various contradictions, and the world is rearranged in accordance.

Furthermore, the themes discussed in connection with acting intuition and the absolute contradictory self-identity are the body, history, art, and life. These are all themes that explicate the theory of *poiesis* in a concrete way. It is significant that Nishida's slogan during this period is changed to *from reality to reality*, or *from the form to the form*. The body, history, art, and life are processes of reality in which forms are actually produced, all the while embodying internal self-contradictions.

The argument that the process of reality cannot be described except from within the process becomes even stronger in this context, where the practical is extracted in a clear manner. This does not mean, however, that the logic of self-awareness, place, and nothingness are abandoned. Rather, these are interwoven into becoming itself. The body, history, art, and life are *forms* which, as contradictory selves, determine themselves in a *self-aware* manner, undergoing a groundless becoming in the face of nothingness, in accordance with the environment called *place*. Here we should understand the struggle experienced by Nishida, who, in order to present the concrete logic of *poiesis* in a precise manner, had no choice but to resort to what may appear as highly abstract jargon. This struggle is, I believe, a difficulty that cannot be avoided when one attempts to describe the act of becoming.

The Core of Nishida's Philosophy

Let us take stock of what we have discussed so far. Nishida sternly rejects the idea that the self can exist as something determinate and detached from the world, something that can survey the truths of the world as if they were already complete. Rather, the self is something that exists within the world; it is something that always has a practical relationship with the world and makes things in concrete acts. Reality cannot be described in any other way. The core of Nishida's philosophy is the attempt to describe this logic of *poiesis* (creating, making) one step at a time, while also explicating the difficulties involved in such a description. Therefore, it is not surprising that Nishida's philosophy can be understood in terms of the key notion of life. For if we concretely suppose there is something that acts but whose acts have no origin or purpose, and which constantly forms itself, then that is nothing other than life. Nishida's theory of *action* can be read directly as a theory of life. The theme of practice can be depicted more vividly in the phenomenon of life than in any other way.

The theory of pure experience is from the outset modeled on the movement of life. It presents the being of life as an organicity. Nishida's theories of self-awareness and place can also be read as something deeply connected with the limitations that life encounters in the face of the infinite, and the relationship between the individual and the environment.

The theory of place is itself posited as a step within the theory of life. The state of absolute nothingness is depicted as leading to a *deep internal life*. Furthermore, there is no doubt that, when Nishida directly discusses *poiesis* in terms of acting intuition and the absolute contradictory self-identity, he is using life as his central model. This is clear from the fact that one of Nishida's late works is entitled "Logic and Life" (1937). He also wrote an essay entitled "Life" in the last period of his life. This last stage can be described as one where Nishida begins using "self-creating" life as the model for existence itself.

Thus, Nishida's philosophy can be read as a philosophy of life that thoroughly depicts the various stages of the theory of life. This kind of reading, I believe, is the kind of reading that elucidates the stage setting and contrivances of Nishida's philosophy. Furthermore, this kind of reading, which presents a theory of life in accordance with its various stages, far from being restricted to the interpretation of Nishida's texts, will provide a significant model for speculations about life today.

Now let us turn to the development of Nishida's philosophy of life, interposing some discussions about the various stages of the theory of life along the way.

1

PURE EXPERIENCE
Aspiration for the Organic One

What Is Pure Experience?

"It is not the case that there is first an individual and then experience; rather, there is first experience and then an individual. Individual experience is merely a peculiar small field determined within experience."[1] These words, from *An Inquiry Into the Good*, clearly display the point of departure and development of Nishida's philosophy.

Pure experience is not my experience. It is not my experience, but it is the foundation by which I realize that there is a world and that I am living in it; and in this sense there is nothing more real. It is not my experience, but something direct and real: this is the "true state of experience as it is in itself," where "the contrivances of the self are completely abandoned, and the facts are followed and known."[2] It is a situation where "there is as yet no subject and no object, where knowledge and its object are completely unified."[3] Philosophy has to start from this kind of situation, which contains from the outset a bit of contradiction.

In general, people often think that "my" experience is what is real. It is often presumed that "my" feelings, "my" thoughts, what "I" see, and what "I" touch are what is real. In philosophical terms, this corresponds to the idea that the world is grasped by self-consciousness; that there is such a thing as the "self" and that the world, as an "object," is discerned by the consciousness possessed by this self.

It is for this reason that notions arise, such as that there is no way of knowing the experience of "others" different from "me," or that "I" am

---

1   *NKZ*, 1: 24.
2   *NKZ*, 1: 9.
3   *NKZ*, 1: 9.

from the outset something unique. Thus, people tend to assume the uniqueness or centrality of the "I" that is different from others. And they speculate about "my" life and death from this kind of perspective of centrality. However, is the experience of the "I" assumed here really something real? It is possible to cast doubt on this notion from various angles. Each of these angles overlaps in some respect with the content of Nishida's theory of pure experience. Let me explain this in broad terms.

When "I" see something, or when "I" feel something, one falls into a quite difficult position if one tries to discern something that can really be said to be "mine." For "me" to see or feel something is always to feel something in the world. The question, then, is: where is this seeing or feeling taking place? Is it taking place somewhere in the world, or in a body that sees and feels? But if the body is an organ wherein feelings take place by sending stimuli to the brain, then is the "I" inside the brain? However, it is difficult to believe that something as special as the "I" is hidden in the brain, which is nothing but a lump of neurons. Where, then, is the "I" that sees and feels? Where are the events that "I" see and feel taking place? Neither of these are self-evident. Furthermore, an important factor here is the fact that insofar as what "I" experience possesses some meaning, it must in large part be a retracing of "someone's" experience.

More fundamentally, is there really something that is seen as peculiar to "me"? May not the very way in which "I" feel something be inexorably imprinted on me by someone else? Furthermore, may not "my" experience be something that inexorably involves the experience of the past "me," which is another person? In this sense, what is seen and felt may be something that is from the outset outside of "my" control.

Philosophy discusses this situation in various ways. The ideas of Nishida and his contemporaries disclose this kind of state that functions prior to the "I."

Nishida's Methodology

For instance, the fact that phenomenology (especially Merleau-Ponty) discusses the impersonal nature of bodily experience is related to this kind of state. By the "impersonal" nature of bodily experience, I am referring to the fundamental way in which our body functions in resonance and cooperation with others, prior to its possessing an explicit consciousness in the form of the "I." Before taking the form of the "I," the body alters its movements in response to objects (for example, upon seeing the color red, the eyeballs may move and the body may alter its posture) and executes its functions in a resonance-like cooperation with others (for example, we often unknowingly imitate the movements of others). Form the standpoint of the "I," these functions take place in a manner that can be characterized as "always already." It is only in *ex post facto* reflection that these bodily functions can be perceived as the functions of a distinct "self." Only in retrospect can we say that these functions are "mine."

And then there is psychoanalysis. What psychoanalysis explicates is the way in which the "unconscious," which is never explicit to "me," always functions as long as "I" live. The "unconscious" is something that exists before the "I" becomes the "I." In particular, psychoanalysis explicates the foundation upon which the life of the "I" in the world is based—a domain that may be characterized as the domain of otherness—by disclosing the realm of "desire."

These discussions that illustrate the impersonality of bodily experience and the unconscious nature of desire are connected with Nishida's pure experience, where the subject and object are undifferenciated, in the sense that they disclose an amalgamated state that functions before the "I" has become the "I," and illustrate the reality of an experience that is not "mine." As mentioned earlier, the fact that these ideas occurred at a point in time that is in some sense the beginning of contemporary philosophy suggests a strong link with Nishida.

However, at the same time we must also note that Nishida's theory of pure experience, which has strong connections with the philosophy of life, displays a subtle divergence from phenomenology and psychoanalysis in terms of methodology. Phenomenology attempts to present the impersonal state in which the body functions by employing the method of phenomenological "reduction," in a sense, from the side of self-consciousness. The impersonal state is thus presented as something prior to reflection, but itself revealed by the operation of reflection. Phenomenology takes the direction of positing a domain of self-consciousness and then seeks to extract the impersonal domain of action as the basis of this self-consciousness (Husserl's notion of *Lebenswelt* clearly expresses this kind of impersonal domain; and Merleau-Ponty follows Husserl methodologically). On the other hand, while psychoanalysis displays the existence of the unconscious in a vivid way, the unconscious is presented as being on the "other side" of, or "external" to, consciousness. Psychoanalysis posits the conscious subject as an origin, so to speak, and attempts to reveal the domain of the unconscious as the invisible outside of this "conscious" subject.

The theory of Nishida, or the philosophy of life, overlaps with phenomenology and psychoanalysis in terms of the phenomena that they focus on, but, as we have seen above, it differs from phenomenology and psychoanalysis in that it does not follow the method of discerning the basis outside of consciousness. Rather, Nishida's (and Bergson's) method goes in the opposite direction. This methodological transition can be said to be what makes the philosophy of life characteristic of contemporary philosophy.

For Nishida (and Bergson), this kind of impersonal domain where the "I" is non-existent is something that is raw and always given in immediacy. That is, this kind of state where the "I" and the world are unified is something that is given from the outset, as if one were thrown into it. And the "I," or the consciousness of the "I," emerges through the determination of this given state, that is, by its function of differentiation. Pure experience is not something that can be discerned in the basis or sought outside of experience. Rather, it is depicted as something positive, something within which we already find ourselves, and from which the "I" and the object are determined. Thus, there is some justification in the view that Nishida's theory of pure experience is in some sense a release from solipsism.

Solipsism is the view that the only thing existing in the world is the "I," that the events of the world are produced by the consciousness of the "I," and that "I" am the center of the world. According to this view, the world exists by virtue of the existence of the "I," and if "I" were to disappear, there would be no meaning in saying that the world exists; to put it in extreme terms, the world itself would disappear. In other words, solipsism is a view that places the "I" at the center of the world in a strong sense, and conceives the existence of the world in terms of the functions of the "I." This view is marked by the idea that the world and other people depend on the existence of the "I."

For Nishida, however, the point of departure is pure experience. The "I" always lives in a state where the "I" cannot be said to be "I," and for the "I" this is what is real. The "I" emerges from within this state; or rather, the consciousness of the "I" branches off as one aspect of such a state: "an individual is nothing but a micro-system within consciousness."[4] Thus, the "I" is not something that constitutes the center from the outset. The "I" is not something original. This does not mean that the "I" lacks content. On the contrary, it is the view that posits the "I" at the center that involves a kind of impoverishment by making the "I" unable to live its experience except as a hollow centrality. The "I" can fulfill its singularity in the true sense only as an aspect of a changing system, namely experience. Yet, in order to explain this sufficiently, we must first attain the requisite vocabulary by tracing the path of Nishida's thinking to its end. Now let us return to the entrance of this path, namely, the theory of pure experience.

The I That Smells a Flower

Let us return to the first stage of pure experience by way of example. I see a flower. It is blossoming in front of my eyes. I smell its scent. There is an "I" that is smelling the scent. That there is an "I" and that there is a scent are one. Here, it is not the case that there is first an "I" that plays the role of a subject smelling the flower. Rather, there is an impersonal state in which the scent is being smelled, prior to "my" smelling the scent. However, neither is it the case that the scent exists in an objective sense, detached from "my" smelling it. It is only by being smelled by someone that it becomes a smell.

The situation of me smelling the scent involves both me and the scent as elements, but the situation itself constitutes a single, intimately connected state. This is what Nishida calls pure experience. The fact that there is a flower emitting a scent, that there is a body feel-

---

ing that scent, and that there is an "I" that plays the role of the body's subject—these are all interwoven into a connected whole, forming pure experience. Each of these states emerges only by the determining dismantlement of pure experience. Therefore, pure experience is neither singular nor complex. It is a single thing that comprises a complex. Pure experience is not something that is experienced by "me." Neither is it something outside of "me." Rather, it is something that contains "me"; it is a "system" of which I can exist only as a part.

An Inquiry into the Good begins with the following words: "to experience means to know facts just as they are."[5] Pure experience is not something that requires some kind of operation in order to be discerned. It is that which we immediately go through. What is important is to refrain from grasping the purity of immediate living from the standpoint of the subjective "I" or from the standpoint of the objective world. Nishida claims that pure experience can be adequately illustrated by "sense experience" and "perception." He writes that any "mental phenomenon," that is, any act of thought, however abstract, is rooted in the immediacy of "sense experience" and "perception." But why should sense experience and perception be more immediate than anything else? Nishida answers by pointing out that sense experience and perception are linked with the "present": "true pure experience has no meaning whatsoever; it is simply the present consciousness of facts just as they are."[6] To be pure is deeply linked with being present, being manifest right in front of one's eyes.

The Body That Climbs a Cliff

What, then, is the "present"? Here Nishida's statement begins approaching a very Bergsonian/Deleuzian theme. Nishida does not regard the present, wherein experience is immediately given, as a point like an instant. Rather, he depicts the present as a state in which a flow is formed. This is close to Bergson's "duration."

---

5   *NKZ*, 1: 9.
6   *NKZ*, 1: 9.

Nishida gives the following examples to illustrate what he means by *flow*: "a climber's determined ascent of a cliff" and "a musician's performance of a piece that has been mastered through practice."[7] The body climbing a cliff must coordinate a series of successive movements into a flow. If one observes each part of the body, one sees that they are all directed toward the single act of climbing. Likewise, in order to perform a musical piece, a musician must move her fingers in such a way that they form the flow of a melody. What we see in both of these instances is a world that emerges as a flow. Although there are various parts involved, they all constitute a flow and move as one. Nishida describes this flow as forming a "continuum of perception."[8] Summarizing these ideas, he writes:

> In these mental phenomena, perception maintains a strict unity and connectedness; when consciousness moves from one thing to another, attention is always directed toward the things perceived and each act gives rise to the next without the slightest crack between them for a thought to enter.[9]

Nishida depicts this "strict unity of concrete consciousness" that is presented by the "continuum of perception" as something that "originally constituted a single system."[10] As a strict unity, the flow is something that constitutes a system. For Nishida, this movement, which is through and through presented as a flow, is a system. What Nishida is saying is as follows: that which is immediately given is the present, and to be present is to be developed within the system of a flow, as exemplified by the coordination of a series of movements or the performance of a musical piece.

To summarize, pure experience is a state of the present where, for example, the "I" that smells the scent of a flower and the scent itself are one. It is a state in which the scent and I form an intimately connected system within the time frame of an instant. The theory of pure experience is further developed by the expansion of the present into a "continuum of perception," where the elements are coordinated into a flow-like movement. The object of perception, which

7   *NKZ*, 1: 11.
8   *NKZ*, 1: 11.
9   *NKZ*, 1: 11.
10   *NKZ*, 1: 11.

is depicted as a flow, and the movement of the conforming body, are thus presented as a system strictly coordinated within the present. But here, we can already see the problems involved in the notion of "purity." Does not the idea of a "present" flow itself express a contradiction? Anything that flows is, in a sense, *ipso facto* not present. It is precisely because of the transition of the present that there can be a flow. It is by virtue of a transition that there can be a system of movement, the performance of a musical piece. Therefore, although pure experience is experience of the present, it is from the outset situated within a temporal succession, in which the present constantly changes itself. But what is regarded as pure experience can only be what is present.

Nishida thus argues that, although pure experience is experience of the present, the present involves a "sphere," and that this sphere changes depending on where one focuses their attention: "the sphere of pure experience will itself coincide with the sphere of attention."[11] Since the present is not an instant, but a flow, it must possess a sphere that overlaps with this flow. But what is this present that possesses a sphere? What kind of determination will this sphere be subject to? Could the breadth of this sphere be indefinite? If one takes into account the notion of the "unified totality" of a system, the breadth of the present should be infinite. Not only that; if all experience is in fact pure experience, then insofar as pure experience is experience of the present, it should be so infinitely broad that it envelops everything.

The sphere of the present expressed by pure experience is indeed flexible. We shall see that this brings huge problems in its wake. But instead of going through these issues in one breath, let us first see what follows from the idea that the present that possesses a sphere forms an indivisible system.

A Heterogeneous and Continuous Flow

This kind of theory regarding the structure of a flow as a transitioning present is a theory that has been developed most sensitively

---

11   *NKZ*, 1: 11.

by Bergson, who treated the phenomenon of pure duration. It also occupies a central place in Deleuze's understanding of Bergson.

Pure duration is a concept introduced by Bergson to describe qualitative, living time (the temporality of experience) as the experience of real time; as opposed to the objective way of reckoning time (the temporality of the clock) that is often reduced to spatiality, and is described as a quantitative juxtaposition. Like Nishida, Bergson discusses pure duration using the example of a melody as his model. A melody is not something that is constituted by a jumble of sounds. In order for a melody to exist as a concrete flow, the individual sounds must be in an intimately connected state. The focus of the theory of pure duration is the issue of how we ought to describe the existence of a flowing system like a melody. In the course of his discussion, Bergson characterizes the nature of a flow as a "heterogeneous continuity." This characterization illustrates the structure of the present that possesses a sphere. The notion of "heterogeneous continuity," which sounds rather peculiar and seems to contain within itself a contradiction, is the key to thinking what Bergson calls "pure duration." What, then, does he mean by "heterogeneous continuity"?

For Bergson, duration, which is a pure state, is an indivisible flow, as exemplified by a melody. An indivisible flow is something that temporally develops itself in mutual interpenetrating connectedness (this flow is what forms the sphere of the present). However, if one spatializes this flowing temporality, then it becomes infinitely divisible, since spatiality is based on the principle of mutually external homogeneity (that is, its qualities remain the same even if one divides it into a jumble of parts).

The nature of space consists in conceiving a flow by fixing it. Through this fixation, it becomes infinitely divisible into minute homogeneous parts. In time, on the other hand, this kind of division can only be something that is cancelled in the reality of flowing movement. Space, however, has an aspect of being abstracted from the movement of the flow. It is through such abstraction that one is able to posit homogeneous units into which space can be infinitely divided. Therefore, if a flow is projected on to space, it is no longer a flow—if one breaks a melody into a jumble of sounds, it is no longer a melody. It is no longer a present that possesses a sphere, but a mere juxtaposition of instants. A flow, being a pure duration, must, prior to being projected on to space, be conceived as a mutually interpenetrating coordination of sounds, a melody. How, then, can we illustrate such a mutual interpenetration?

Faced with this question, Bergson characterized the flow of duration as a temporal manifold wherein heterogeneous elements are continuous, in the sense that it cannot be grasped in terms of a homogeneous spatiality. A mutually interpenetrating flow is something that cannot be reduced to something homogeneous; it is formed by the interweaving of heterogeneous elements and in turn forms a single system. This kind of "heterogeneous continuity" presents a logic that is necessary in thinking about systems in general that can be described as a flow. Let us consider this next, in order to attain a deeper understanding of the meaning of heterogeneous continuity.

What is it that is coordinated into a flow? It is the movements of the body that climbs a cliff, the movements involved in the performance of a musical piece, the "continuum of perceptions." It is this that is conceived as a flowing system. In this context, for the elements of a flow to be a mutually interpenetrating existence, they must fit within the sphere of the present and be incapable of separation into discrete elements. It is only when the temporal flow is projected on to a homogeneous space that the elements of a flow become discrete.

However, just as a melody that is broken into a jumble of sounds is no longer a melody, the juxtaposition of discrete elements (instants) is no longer a flow. The coordination of elements must be presented as a mutual containment, inseparable into homogeneous parts. This kind of inseparable mutual containment indicates the mutual interpenetration of heterogeneous elements. This inseparable mutual containment is thus depicted as a system consisting of a multiplicity of heterogeneous elements that rejects homogeneity. It is a manifold, a heterogeneous continuity. For Bergson and Deleuze, this term describes the being of the flow itself. Likewise, it describes Nishida's pure experience, which is an intimately connected system.

A System That Has Its Own Aspect of Distinction

If one reads Nishida's texts with such an awareness of the issues, the focal point of his discussion becomes apparent. The focal point are the notions of *differentiation* and *differenciation*, which are the ways in which the heterogeneity and multiplicity of a flow presents itself; but also, *virtuality*, which is the mode of being of the heterogeneous elements. What, then, are differenciation and virtuality? This statement from Nishida will provide us with the first step of our examination: "like any organic entity, a system of consciousness manifests its wholeness through the orderly, differenciated development of a certain unifying reality."[12] Let us recall that pure experience indicates a movement where the subject and object are undifferenciated, and is in this sense an impersonal flow. And this flow, as a heterogeneous continuity, constitutes a system.

Nishida describes this system as something like an organic entity, which is formed by its elements being mutually dependent on each other (as I will discuss later, the body of a living organism can be described as a mutual coordination of elements). In one respect, this system takes on an undifferenciated state, that is, a state where "the facts are perceived just as they are, and are thought to be without meaning." On the other hand, it is a system where various meanings and judgments arise through the "distinction" of experience. That is, it is a system that "has its own aspect of distinction."[13] Therefore, the state of pure experience plays the role of a place from which individual meanings and judgments arise, through its differenciation.

For example, when one says that "a horse is running," pure experience plays the role of the representation of a running horse that makes such a linguistically articulated judgment possible.[14] At the stage of the judgment, the subject "horse" and the predicate "is running" are clearly distinct. But in pure experience, the "running horse" itself is presented immediately, without any separation between the domain of subject and the domain of predicate. But this does not mean that what is presented is molten into an undifferentiated whole. The "run-

---

12   *NKZ*, 1: 12.
13   *NKZ*, 1: 13.
14   *NKZ*, 1: 16.

ning horse" is a movement that possesses an "aspect of distinction" (difference) by which the subject "horse" and predicate "is running" can be discriminated. Pure experience is given immediately as something that possesses this kind of aspect of distinction.

A judgment is a differentiated explication of this pure experience that possesses an aspect of distinction. Both a melody and the movement of a body climbing a cliff can be articulated linguistically in a judgment. Such an articulation is based on the differenciation and actualization of the pure experience that is given immediately within a flow. What, then, is the mode of being of this aspect of distinction possessed by pure experience itself? What is the nature of a difference that is immanent within an indivisible flow?

The Virtual

Here, we run into the concept of *virtuality*. This is a concept that had great significance for both Bergson and Deleuze in their ontological explications of the heterogeneous continuity. Nishida describes the aspect of distinction immanent within pure experience using terms such as "implicative" and "virtual": "this representation [representation of "pure experience"], which was acting from the beginning in an implicative manner, reaches a judgment when it becomes actual";[15] "both volition and knowledge can be regarded as the systematic development of something virtual."[16]

The virtual is the foundation upon which pure experience differenciates itself and develops into something actual. But the virtual itself can never be explained in terms of the actual. In this sense, the virtual is a mode of being that constitutes the reality of a flow. Let us consider this in concrete terms. Listening to the flow of a melody is pure experience. Each sound within the melody constitutes a system with the other sounds. It is for this reason that the series of sounds is heard as melody. To say that a flow actualizes is, in one respect, to say that this experience of listening to a melody differenciates itself,

---

15   *NKZ*, 1: 16.
16   *NKZ*, 1: 16.

so that each sound can be heard. However, the sounds within a flow do not exist as individual sounds. While they possess an aspect of distinction (difference), they exist as a unified whole. This is the present that possesses a sphere. If attention is paid to the melody itself, the act of hearing the entire totality would be the present. What, then, is the nature of the individual sounds that intimately connect with each other to form a flow? They are elements such that if they are extracted as individuals (differentiated, actualized), they no longer form a melody. Yet the sounds that are capable of becoming individual sounds are "aspects of distinction" within the flow. That is, they are contained within the flow from the beginning, as something that forms a heterogeneous difference. This kind of differentiation that grounds the differenciation of individual events is virtuality.

The systematic nature of a flow must be conceived as originating in virtual differences. It must be discerned as a heterogeneity that is no longer a flow when it is differentiated and actualized, but virtually contains differences within itself. To put it plainly, these virtual differences are modes of force. A force is something that itself appears as real, but becomes a mere trace when grasped in the realm of actuality. In order to discern the force itself, one must seek the state where the virtual force lines intertwine, prior to its actualization and differenciation. The mode of such a force is, to use Nishida's words again, an "internal dunamis."[17] It is a system whose development allows us to conceive of volition and knowledge.

In order to view Nishida's discussion so far from a different perspective, let us consider it in connection with Bergson's philosophy of life. There is a strong tendency in Bergson to view these forces, these virtual differences, as indeterminacies that produce change, as something positively indeterminable. It is for this reason that Bergson uses the development and evolution of life as a model for thinking about existence. For him, a virtual force is an indeterminacy that weaves together the multiplicity of the actual world by differentiating itself in multifarious ways. This tendency is also shared by Nishida.

Furthermore, both Bergson (in the third chapter of *Matter and Memory*) and Nishida share the tendency to overlay this domain of

---

17   *NKZ*, 1: 26.

virtuality onto the theory of conceptual universality, through the notion of judgment (in Nishida, this becomes especially perspicuous in the theory of place, which I will discuss later). That is, Nishida directly describes the virtual as the "universality of concepts itself."[18] The virtual thus appears as a "totality" or universal that lies as a background against which individuals are realized. Nishida writes: "The true universal is a *dunamis* that lies behind individual realization ... it is something like the seed of a plant."[19]

The domain of the concept that is suffused with the force of universality overlaps with the model of a flow-like virtuality. And Nishida describes this domain using the biological metaphor of the seed. The seed is a symbol of that which is filled with various virtual forces, but is itself undifferentiated. The seed can be actualized and concretized in various ways. The basic driving force that produces these actualizations is contained within the seed, as something that bears the property of indeterminacy—a property not possessed by anything actual. The seed is thus a typical example of a mode of force within the domain of life.

The Aspiration and Trap of Becoming One

So far, we have seen what Nishida means by the virtuality of the system of pure experience by examining the notion of differenciation. However, there is one other topic that is strongly linked to the notion of a virtual system, which is the realm of totality that is contained within the virtual system. The theory of differenciation discusses the nature of the heterogeneity that is implied in the continuous. Now we will consider the infinity of connections presupposed by the continuous. The theme here will be the "single system"[20] possessed by the virtual, the "single unifying force" that lies at "the basis of the universe and all existence."[21]

A virtual system forms pure experience itself. However, as I mentioned earlier, the sphere of this pure experience can expand indefinitely

---

18   *NKZ*, 1: 22.
19   *NKZ*, 1: 22.
20   *NKZ*, 1: 57.
21   *NKZ*, 1: 63.

according to the scope of attention. The present, it will be recalled, can have an infinite breadth, depending on which aspect of the (in principle) infinitely continuous flow to which one pays attention. This is one of the difficulties that the theory of pure experience faces.

Let us think about this. Pure experience is an indivisible flow. Insofar as it is indivisible, there must in principle be an infinity both before and after the flow. Furthermore, the flow is something virtual. The limit of the continuous is not something that can be actualized. Therefore, if we think of the flow as something virtual, this "limit" must itself be capable of being grasped by the model of virtuality. And insofar as the logic of an indivisible flowing system necessarily implies thinking of the indefinitely expandable connection hidden within itself, this kind of model is inevitable. Here we meet the realm of the "totality" or "one"—or, in other words, a certain virtual "unifying reality" possessed by pure experience. If we think of an indivisibly connected flow, the limit of such a flow must also manifest itself as something virtual. If we attempt to describe this something, it should be described as a totality or one that contains the entirety of the infinitely connected flow called reality. If individual events are intimately connected as a flow that cannot be conceived as a jumble, then we must presuppose a totality or one as the ultimate form of this connection.

There are two points that should be highlighted in Nishida's discussion above. The first is that Nishida never conceives of unity in terms of actualization or differenciation. The totality is through and through regarded as a process that is involved in continuous, virtual action. For example, Nishida discusses unity in the contexts of thought, volition, and acting intuition (which approach the reality of the flow in this order): "consciousness is originally a unified system. Its natural state is to develop and perfect itself. ... In short, thought is nothing but the process of a great system of consciousness developing and realizing itself";[22] "[a]s a fact of pure experience, there is no distinction between volition and knowledge; both are processes of a certain universal being systematically realizing itself. The limit of

---

this unification is at once truth and action";[23] "[b]ut true intellectual intuition is nothing but the unifying act in pure experience itself; it is the grasping of life."[24]

In each of these contexts, Nishida assumes that there is a unified one. But he does not regard this as an actualization of a flow. Rather, it is regarded as that which captures the continuity of the flow itself, as the limit of the process. It is depicted from a perspective that tries to discern the totality of a dynamic and coordinated movement that forms a system and develops itself. The ultimate form of thought, that which volition strives towards, and that which is attained by acting intuition—the power of conforming oneself with the reality of a flow—is the one that develops as a virtual process. It is here that the virtual totality presents itself.

However, there is one other point that ought to be noted. It is that Nishida's theory of the totality remains half-baked. And this weakness can be said to be a fundamental bottleneck in Nishida's conception of the totality as the system of a flow. For example, at the end of Part Two of *An Inquiry Into the Good*, Nishida writes: "God, who is the unity of the universe, is indeed the basis of this unified action."[25] The "reality that is God" is the name Nishida gives to the "infinite" that arises when a flow, as a continuum, reaches infinity. This is an act of assuming a unifier of the infinite process and giving it a name.

Furthermore, regarding the notion of the "Good" that appears in the title of the book, *An Inquiry Into the Good*, there is a strong tendency in Nishida to depict the Good as a movement of virtual forces towards unity or God. This development, which brings in God as the "basis of reality" and consolidates various ideas into this entity, all the while presenting the process of the flow as a unity, gives the impression of being a very hasty move.[26] Although Nishida presents the totality that is assumed to lie in the background of the indivisible continuity as a process, he does not explain why this origin of forces should bear the name "one." Furthermore, it seems that with

23   *NKZ*, 1: 29.
24   *NKZ*, 1: 35.
25   *NKZ*, 1: 82.
26   *NKZ*, 1: 142.

this move, he is evading the logical *aporia* involved in the infinite development of virtuality.

While Nishida regards the end of a virtual flow as a dynamic process, he concretizes this as the one. This structure of the theory presented in *An Inquiry Into the Good* is deeply linked with the issue of the present that pure experience involves. For Nishida's theory is the outcome of inferring, from the circumstance that the present has an indefinite sphere depending on how attention is paid, that the infinite totality is a simple expansion of the pure experience of the present. But this does nothing but confine the issue of the infinite virtuality into a single plane. That is, this theory is unable to capture the paradoxical nature of the totality, which is something virtual and cannot be discerned in actualization, in the dynamism of the phenomena.

An Inquiry into the Good as a Theory of Organic Relations

What would the theory in *An Inquiry Into the Good* look like when viewed as a stage within a theory of life? It would appear as a typical model of a theory of organic relations. What is it that Nishida wants to show with his notion of organic relations? This notion plays an effective role whenever we want to distinguish organic life from something mechanical. In one respect, life is a machine made of matter. It is therefore through and through subordinate to material functions. However, it does not take much thought to realize that the peculiarity of life phenomena cannot be explained by reducing life to material elements. Connecting the matter that constitutes the individual parts of a body does not make it a living thing. It is only when each part forms an organically integrated system that the body becomes a living thing.

Life possesses the power to develop itself. Life self-replicates, self-develops, and evolves. Life exhibits forces of propagation, diversification, and self-organization that cannot be captured by the simple material laws of reductionism. A perspective is always necessary that can grasp this character of life. How can we illustrate such a perspective?

The first idea that was presented was the idea that organic entities simply oppose the mechanical. The idea was to focus on the organic relations that constitute the content of organic entities. What is important in organic entities is the priority of relations over elements, or the priority of the whole over the parts. Take, for example, a cell of the body. In order for it to function as life, it must work in mutual relation within the overall system. The functions of life derive their meaning solely from a conglomeration of relationships, such as the relation with the living organism as a whole, other living organisms, and the surrounding environment. Life is distinguished from matter by the fact that it is a subject with these kinds of organic relations.

Both Bergson's pure duration and Nishida's pure experience can be regarded as philosophical variations of this kind of theory of organic life. The theories of pure experience and pure duration both attempt to capture the world just as it is, prior to the separation of subject and "object." When I see a flower and smell its scent, I am one with the flower. Bergson and Nishida's theories both attempt to grasp this fundamental realm of experience. In this realm, not only is the relation between the subject and object described as undifferentiated, but the world is also a flow. That is, the theories of pure experience and pure duration both depict an indivisible continuity, prior to its being sundered into elements. Everything is described as being a single organically linked system. Everything is grasped as a continuous flow that cannot be reduced to discrete elements.

These theories can be said to directly provide a model of organic relations. Both Bergson and Nishida emphasize psychological sensations and feelings in their writings during this period. Yet, as evinced by the used of the adjective "living," this emphasis is from the outset linked with an account of life.

The Paradox of Holism

This kind of discussion contains from the outset an internal problem. Let us review this issue, which I have already pointed out at the end of our discussion of *An Inquiry Into the Good*. The issue is linked with the question: what is the limit of the relationships assumed in Nishida's theory?

The gist of the theory of organic entities was the idea that the whole is prior to its parts. The comprehensive entity gives meaning to the activity of the parts. But let us think about this. What is the "whole" in this context? Of course, it cannot be something that is visible to the eye or appears with a definite shape. If the whole were something visible or something that appears with a definite shape, then it would itself be only a part that constitutes the world. A whole that is grasped in actuality in this way is immediately brought back to the realm of the elements. The whole is, therefore, something that cannot be conceived as actual. If we think of the whole in this way, then it would entail the infinite expansion of relationships. But what is the infinite expansion that results in this way?

There is a tendency in theories of "purity" to regard the infinite expansion of relationships, or the whole, as a flat expansion of the experience of the present. They posit the present as a "fixed point" and depict the whole as an expansion of this fixed point. As a textual issue, this is linked with the act of expanding a psychological account (an account that depicts a model of relationships) immediately to a cosmological level. This kind of tendency can also be discerned in *An Inquiry Into the Good*. However, can we correctly grasp the whole in such a manner? Does not such an approach involve a kind of danger? The danger is that the theory that prioritizes relations may fall into a simplistic holism. Holism is a philosophy that hypostatizes the "whole" that can only be presented as infinite, and thereby defines the individual from the side of this hypostatized whole. This is a consequence of depicting the whole as if it were a single thing by expanding the present, as in the case of Nishida. Here, the whole, which is something that cannot be depicted as being actual, is manipulated as if it were an actual thing, and the value of individual, which is a part of this whole, seems to be uniquely determined.

Such a theory can be said to be a theory of organic relations that has abandoned its task of depicting its own infinite limit as a process, and posits the limit as something that exists somewhere. This is typical of theories that discuss the organic connectedness of life as opposed to life as an individual, and posits a "life in general" that governs this connectedness. The infinity of relationships is not something that can be hypostatized in any form. It must be regarded as a whole upon which the parts depend, but which itself is infinitely open. The move that hypostatizes the "whole" stipulates this openness as something closed.

If one posits the "whole" of a flow as in holism, where the individuals are the differentiated elements must always be regarded as subordinate to the whole. In the political context, this leads to a kind of totalitarianism. An ethical theory that naïvely regards the earth as Gaia (a single organism) involves the same kind of logic. This logic presupposes a "whole" that cannot be depicted. Insofar as the whole itself can only be grasped as a developing virtual process, the act of depicting the whole involves a kind of paradox. Both Nishida and Bergson's theories of purification have a strong tendency towards an organic holism. This tendency becomes especially conspicuous when one emphasizes the opposition of the model of life against reductionism.

Both Nishida and Bergson critically reflect upon this tendency in the development of their thought. When Nishida discusses self-awareness he will take issue with the infinity of relationships and update his own ideas. This is also linked with the development of a theory of life itself.

2

THE FUNCTION OF SELF-AWARENESS
Self-Determination Within Infinity

The Introduction of Self-Awareness

Normally, self-awareness is understood as one's awareness of oneself. It is the act of reflecting on oneself, of reevaluating one's place. This is what is normally meant by self-awareness. Nishida's theory of self-awareness also involves this normal sense of the term. However, we must keep in mind that, for Nishida, who argues from the perspective of pure experience, there is no such thing as a previously given domain of the "self." Self-awareness is then not the act of discerning a pre-existing "self." Rather, it is the act of creating (actualizing from a virtual state) the "I" and the "world" by distinguishing them within the pure experience that lives according to an infinite flow.

Self-awareness is a term that was introduced by Nishida that indicates how we should consider the infinity of relationships within pure experience. It is a term that refers to the act whereby concrete events arise through determination within the pure experience that lives an infinite flow. In this sense, self-awareness is the self-determination of experience within infinity. Nishida discusses self-awareness mainly in a book entitled, *Intuition and Reflection in Self-Awareness*, which consists of forty odd short fragments. His book *The Problem of Consciousness* (1920) will also be helpful in this connection.

Like all of Nishida's books that were written after *An Inquiry Into the Good*, it is very difficult to see at first what the main topic of *Intuition and Reflection in Self-Awareness* is about. Nishida himself described the work as "the document of a hard-fought battle";[1] and indeed, one can see that in this book he is re-examining his own theory of the system

---

1   *NKZ*, 2: 11.

that he had attained in his theory of pure experience. The discussion of the book proceeds while incorporating various contemporaneous ideas, such as those of Fichte, Neo-Kantianism, and Bergson. Through trial and error, Nishida develops the issues involved in pure experience in various directions.

The texts on self-awareness are, therefore, especially intricate. They contain in germinal form many of the arguments that Nishida will clearly develop in his later years. However, in order to disentangle these intricate arguments, I will focus on two points. The first is the question of what self-awareness is; namely, what is the peculiar logical structure that self-awareness possesses? The second point is the question: why was it necessary for Nishida to tenaciously engage with the mathematical theories of the differential, infinity, and set theory in thinking about the logic of self-awareness? My aim is to show, through an examination of these two points, how Nishida reconceived the issues of the present and the infinite that he had faced in his reflections on pure experience.

What Is Self-Awareness?

At the beginning of *Intuition and Reflection in Self-Awareness*, Nishida introduces the topic of self-awareness by discussing the themes of "intuition" and "reflection":

> Intuition is an ever-progressing consciousness where subject and object are undifferentiated, where the knower and known are one, and where reality is just as it is. Reflection is a consciousness that stands outside of this progression and sees it from afar ... I think that it is our self-awareness that allows us to see the internal relation between these two states.[2]

Reading this, we see that self-awareness is conceived in connection with intuition and reflection. Here, *intuition* is the act of living pure experience, of uniting oneself with the reality of the infinite flow. It refers to a way of grasping things in accordance with the temporal flow itself. The indivisible flow is discerned as the flow itself by

---

2   *NKZ*, 2: 13.

intuition. On the other hand, *reflection* is the act of reconceiving the experience of the temporal flow in a spatial manner.[3] It is the act of detaching oneself from living the flow itself and re-grasping the flow. Reflection is this kind of re-grasping of the flow. What is important here, however, is that even in reflection it is impossible to separate oneself from the "reality of intuition,"[4] as if one were making a map of the flow from the sky. That is, reflection cannot be detached from the movement of the flow.

Self-awareness is introduced as something that connects intuition and reflection. It is the link between the infinite living of intuition and the reflection that re-grasps it. Let me rephrase this. To be in a state of pure experience is to be completely within a flow. It is to live a state of virtuality, which is a force of differentiation. Reflection, which takes the form of spatialization, can then be understood as the differenciation and actualization of this virtuality. Through such reflection, the forces of differentiation manifest themselves and become clear.

The act of re-grasping, however, can only be performed from within the flow. That is, it can only be an act of determining infinite differences from within the infinity of the flow. Nishida, therefore, argues that self-awareness is an "infinitely progressing" or "act of self-development."[5] Self-awareness is an "act" that actualizes the system of pure experience and further develops it as a flow in accordance with pure experience.

Nishida's Self-Awareness and Bergson's Pure Duration

In order to consider the logic of self-awareness, let us examine its overlap with Bergson's theory of pure duration. As we have seen, for Bergson, pure duration is an indivisible continuity. Therefore, even when one is depicting the individual "I" or an individual object, these are always conceived of as arising from the basis of a continuous flow.

A typical logic that displays this development is the logic of dissociation that is taken up in the contexts of perception and memory.

---

3   *NKZ*, 2: 13.
4   *NKZ*, 2: 13.
5   *NKZ*, 2: 13.

Regarding this, Bergson writes roughly as follows. Let us consider, for instance, the recollection of an image from an infinite string of memories. In traditional psychology, this is understood in terms of "association." The theory of association is the theory that there are pre-existing individual images, and that these images are connected together and actualized through the operation of some logic (such as resemblance or contiguity). According to this theory, the recollection of a certain memory occurs through the discernment of a resembling memory or contiguous situation. For instance, the recollection of a certain person is made possible by (externally) linking together various elements pertaining to that person.

Bergson, however, does not employ this kind of idea of association. Memory is from the outset a virtual, mutually interpenetrating, connected series. The memory of a certain person is like a nebula; it is situated within a virtual (internal) network of various memories pertaining to that person. Recollecting is to disentangle this intricate network. The association of memories is, therefore, nothing but a logic of the re-structuring of memories that have already been differentiated and actualized. What we must consider is how, prior to this, an image could have been virtually connected with countless other images. We must dive immediately, so to speak, into the network of images. That is, when something arises, what we must explain is not how the image becomes concretized through connections (associations). It is rather the opposite. Everything that exists in this world is already connected with everything else. To exist within a flow of relationships is to bear the infinity of virtual relationships.

Thus, what is most important for the transformation of memory into an image is the act that disentangles the connections within the virtual state, so that something individual can be extracted. It is the act whereby something is dissociated as an individual from the domain of undifferentiated differences. What we must inquire into is the mechanism of dissociation within infinity. Nishida's theory of self-awareness is deeply linked with this problem discussed by Bergson.

For Nishida, pure experience is a flow where the subject and object are undifferentiated. Thus, there is no "I" that is presupposed, nor are there any "objects" on this side of the world. However, in order for this undifferentiated and continuous flow to act as something concrete, it must somehow determine and unfold itself. Otherwise, there would be no way for the infinitely continuous pure experience to actualize its differences. This actualization through determination is none other than self-reflection. The "I," which is a single moment of the flow, arises as something reflective; and likewise, the world itself, which was presented as a flow, becomes actualized as something individual in the determination of the flow through reflection: "experience determines itself. That which is determined is objective; the act that determines itself, i.e., that act of dissociation, is subjective."[6]

The "I" is something that appears through this kind of reflection. Likewise, various objects arise through actualization. Both the "I" and objects are objective entities that are determined in this manner. Nishida says that the act of dissociation that performs this determination is subjective. Here, the reflection that extracts virtual differences and actualizes them overlaps, as an act, with the intuition that grasps the flow. It is this overlapping that Nishida tried to capture through his theory of self-awareness.

The Infinite Development of Self-Awareness

The significance of the fact that Nishida developed his theory of self-awareness as an extension of the theory of pure experience will become clearer when we view it from the perspective of the determination of infinity. We will thus see that his theory of self-awareness was, in a way, an attempt to re-conceptualize the difficulty involved in the theory of pure experience, the difficulty of simply expanding presentism, that is, the problem of depicting the "whole" as a hypostatization through the simple expansion of the present. We will also see the infinitely broad virtuality of pure experience, as well as the interplay between this virtuality and actuality.

Here, let us examine in more detail how intuition and reflection overlap in self-awareness. The act of reflection that actualizes events cannot itself be detached from the infinite act of intuition. Rather, it is something that drives this infinite act. This is related to Nishida's

---

6   *NKZ*, 2: 56.

description of self-awareness in terms of the development of a mechanism that "mirrors itself within itself":

> The self's reflection on itself, its mirroring itself, does not yet come to an end at this point, for it consists of an infinite process of unification .... When the self reflects on itself or mirrors itself, it does not do so detached from the self, as when experience is mirrored in the form of concepts. Rather, the self mirrors itself within itself.[7]

> Whatever differentiates and develops in this way does not acquire force from the outside. Rather, the self-same one mirrors itself within itself ... That is, consciousness is a process in which the virtual totality develops itself. Of course, we cannot immediately say that the virtual one and manifest one are identical; but our immediate experience is such an endless process of fluctuation of consciousness.[8]

Nishida is saying two things here. The first is that, since self-awareness is the act of determining pure experience, its nature is to "mirror itself within itself." Therefore, ostensibly there arises a distinction between the "virtual" self, wherein the act of "mirroring" (intuiting) takes place, and the "manifest" self, which is "mirrored" (reflected). The act of determination in self-awareness consists in the arising of this manifest (actual) something.

But what is even more important here is that this act of reflection in self-awareness can only function within the dynamic network of pure experience. The act of reflection is not a movement from pure experience to something else. The actual thing that arises through reflection is not something utterly external, like a mere object or concept. Rather, the act of actualization itself again gives rise to virtuality (and hence, differences). Thus, self-awareness forms an "infinite series."

Drawing a Map That Depicts Oneself

Nishida's following account will be helpful in considering the dynamic identity of self-awareness. Citing the American philosopher

---

7   *NKZ*, 2: 13–14.
8   *NKZ*, 2: 55.

Josiah Royce, he gives the following example: "suppose one were in the United Kingdom and planned to make a complete map of that country."[9] To draw a complete map of the UK from within the UK, and hence to draw a map that depicts oneself, is analogical to the act of actualizing oneself in self-awareness. To draw this kind of map, the act of drawing itself would have to be reflected in what is drawn. Thus, "each realization of this plan would immediately give rise to the project of drawing another, even more complete map,"[10] resulting in an infinite process. Again, Nishida writes that "an object between two mirrors reflects its figure infinitely."[11] In this kind of act, the actualization that arises through self-awareness again generates new differences in the domain of virtuality, thus endlessly demanding further actualizations.

Bergson also discusses the interplay between virtuality and actuality using the image of the mirror.[12] Furthermore, Deleuze, in his *Cinema*, cites Bergson's theory and discusses the indistinguishability of virtuality and actuality. Both of these accounts discuss the difficulty of overlaying the present (the actualized), due to its being present, directly on to the flow (the virtual). In Nishida's theory of self-awareness, the present is no longer depicted as something that is flatly expanded to infinity. Rather, the present is a place of dynamic acts, where the virtual and actual resonate with each other.

For Bergson, the past (the virtual) is something that possesses a "difference in nature" from the present (the actual). The past is not something that has once become present and then is transformed, for instance, by a psychological reduction of its force (in that case, there would only be a "difference of degree" between the two). Rather, according to Bergson, the present is something that is cancelled within the flow. The present can also be characterized as a mere peak of the past (virtuality) that constitutes the major part of the flow. Therefore, in contrasting the past and present, Bergson rejects the

---

9   *NKZ*, 2: 14.
10 *NKZ*, 2: 14.
11 *NKZ*, 2: 14.
12 Bergson, Henri, "Le souvenir du présent et la fausse reconnaissance," in *L'Énergie spirituelle: Essais et conférences* (Paris: Félix Alcan, 1919), English translation in *Mind-Energy: Lectures and Essays*, trans. H. Wildon Carr (London: McMillan and Company, 1920).

view that places the present at the center, and instead regards the present as a single phase of the actualization of the past (virtuality), and thus, as something of a "different nature" from the past.

But in that case, how does the past (virtuality) itself arise? If the present is regarded as the peak of the flow (the virtual past), then the question becomes: how did the past come into being? Here, Bergson argues that, in the progression of the flow, the present and past are two different directions that are differentiated by "splitting." And in order to illustrate this differentiation of directions, he employs the metaphor of the mirror. The virtual is an image of the actual reflected on the surface of a mirror. He describes the present as a place where images simultaneously split into the actual and virtual.

However, what if we reconceive of this present within the flow? In that case, the actual would itself can only be something that arises from the determination of the virtual. Thus, are not actuality and virtually two things that reciprocally mirror each other, as if they were grasping each other's tail? (This is none other than Deleuze's theme of the indistinguishability of the actual and virtual).

This overlaps with the infinite act of drawing a map that depicts oneself. The virtual and actual that bifurcate at the peak of the present cannot be captured by the merely static framework of an object in front of a mirror and the image of that object in the mirror. Insofar as the actual itself arises through the determination of the virtual, this mirror scheme cannot be regarded as anything but an infinitely progressing mutual reflection of actuality and virtuality.

In this sense, self-awareness should be understood as the place of an infinite act. Nishida's theory of self-awareness does not deal with a mere present that has a sphere, as in his theory of pure experience. Rather, it extracts the moving, infinite reflection of actualization/ virtualization as the process of pure experience itself. Self-awareness, which is itself the production of infinity, unfolds its structure on the basis of pure experience. The theory of self-awareness reexamines the presentism of pure experience in the context of the infinitely dynamical. Here, one gets a glimpse into the issue of the infinitude of the flow, an issue that cannot be grasped by the idea of simply expanding the present. This infinitude becomes the next focal point of Nishida's thought.

The Differential and the Theory of Infinity

We have seen how the theory of self-awareness steps into the issue of the continuity of flowing reality in a dynamic way. This theory forces us to further inquire into the related issue of infinity. In order to discuss this subject, Nishida during this period refers frequently to the differential calculus and set theory, that is, mathematical ideas that deal with infinity.

Notwithstanding the general image of Nishida as a religious philosopher who developed an Eastern philosophy of nothingness, references to mathematics and science comprise a considerable portion of his corpus. There was a period in which he aspired to be a mathematician, and he was well-acquainted with mathematical discussions. Furthermore, Neo-Kantianism[13] which Nishida had been studying at the time, frequently employed mathematical arguments (references to Cohen constitute the major part of Nishida's mathematical discussions). And above all else, it was a period of fluidity, when fundamental revolutions were taking place in the foundations of mathematics (Nishida frequently refers to Georg Cantor, who developed set theory, the foundation of mathematics). There is no doubt that all of these factors contributed to sharpening Nishida's mathematical ideas.

The use of mathematics is especially conspicuous in *Intuition and Reflection in Self-Awareness* and *The Problem of Consciousness*. This is in a sense inevitable, given that the theory of self-awareness, as I mentioned earlier, must deal with the infinitude of the continuum of the flow in a dynamic way.

Let us begin by considering the relation between self-awareness and the differential. Nishida writes as follows (here, x is a variable, and dx is an ideal infinitesimal that constitutes the ground of the mathematical differentiation; usually it is written in the form dy/dx):

> For a sense quality to be perceived, there must be something universal as the basis of that perception. And that universal ... must be something immanent within experience. It must be something like dx in relation to x in mathematics. This is

---

13　Neo-Kantianism is a late nineteenth century school of thought that sought to revive Kant's epistemology. Nishida frequently cites Hermann Cohen, founder of the Marburg school of Neo-Kantianism.

probably why the Marburg School understands the infinitesimal to be the basis of reality. Just as we regard dx as the foundation of finite x in analysis, so we perceive a given sense quality as the determination of a continuous totality ....[14]

We can think of a finite curve as arising from an infinitesimal point; we can think of dx as the origin of x ... Can we not understand the relation between our finite consciousness and the infinite unconsciousness that lies at its base in terms of the relation between the finite and infinite, in the sense described above? Can we not understand the unconsciousness that lies behind our finite consciousness as something like dx in relation to x?[15]

What is it that Nishida is trying to say when employing this notion of the differential? He is trying to describe the form by which the finite (actual) arises from the infinite (virtual) as a determination of self-awareness.

Nishida continues his discussion of the differential in a concrete way by taking up the consciousness of straight lines and the consciousness of colors. Any real straight line is infinite (by definition, if it is not infinite then it is not a straight line). However, when we become conscious of the straight line, we are subjecting the infinity of the line to determination. It is by subjecting the infinitely expanding virtual line to determination that we are able to conceive of it as a finite, actual line.[16] This is the structure of consciousness. But behind consciousness, unconsciousness is enclosed, so to speak.

Again, colors come in an infinite multitude of variations. Behind the existence of any color lies the bloom and buzz of an infinity of colors. But in order to become conscious of any color, that color must be actualized from color in itself, which possesses an infinite multitude of implications.[17] That is, determination must take place. This kind of determination has an infinite multitude of variations as its backdrop.

It is pure experience, as intuition, that feels this kind of infinite line or infinite color. It is something like "an artist with pure vision seeing a curve within a straight line, or a tendency towards black and white within every color."[18] It signifies the dx of mathematical dif-

---

14   *NKZ*, 2: 77.
15   *NKZ*, 2: 86.
16   *NKZ*, 2: 107.
17   *NKZ*, 2: 100.
18   *NKZ*, 2: 100.

ferentiation because it is infinite. This dx is something that we cannot become conscious of in a clear way, but we become aware of its existence by existing within it. But when we try to grasp it as something distinct, it flies away. It is something real and given in immediacy, but insofar as it is invisible, it can only be described as something "ideal."

In contrast, consciousness, that is, the appearance of something by way of self-awareness, is the determination of that something from a state of immersion into the infinite variation; it is the x in relation to dx. It is the establishing of something concrete, as opposed to the idea. It is the establishment and actualization of a center within an infinite flow.

Here, one must bear in mind that, for Nishida, what is real is the infinite dx. What is real is the continuous idea. The colors and straight lines that one sees are not real. These are mere aspects of reality. In other words, since the real straight lines and real colors are infinitely connected, we cannot see them with our eyes. They are invisible, ideal things. To make them visible is to extract reality from a certain perspective and determine it. Through determination, a straight line becomes a visible thing, and a color becomes present to consciousness. But this also causes the infinity implied in experience to be scraped off. This kind of "finitude" is what is taking place in self-awareness, our concrete acts of consciousness.

Deleuze presents a theory parallel to that of Nishida described above. In *Difference and Repetition*, he illustrates the indeterminate forces of differentiation by using the mathematical concept of the differential. The task of his ontology of becoming is to give an account of how events differenciate through mathematical differentiation.

From Infinity to Intensive Magnitude/Intensity

These discussions can be said to fall within the sphere of the theme of intensive magnitude. What is intensive magnitude? It is a magnitude that is presented in contrast to extensive magnitude. It is the reality of the heterogeneous and continuous flow that was presented by Bergson. An extensive magnitude is a magnitude formed by a collection of mutually external parts, a magnitude that can be measured by homogeneous and spatial divisions. It is a whole made by a piling up of parts. In contrast, intensive magnitude is something qualitative that develops in mutual interpenetration within the flow; it is a magnitude that forms a heterogeneous manifold and expresses the indivisible continuity of time. Intensive magnitude is something that can only be discerned in such a way that the whole is prior to its parts, which arise through determination from the totality. In this sense, intensive magnitude, to use Cohen's phrase, is a "continuous production."[19]

The theory of intensive magnitude, as a way of illustrating the ideal infinite force—a force that is real and given in immediacy but is itself invisible—links with the theory of the differential. Intensive magnitude, according to Nishida, was taken up by Kant, but was not yet made clear by him. The significance of intensive magnitude was first made clear by Cohen and his treatment of the differential.[20] Both Nishida and Deleuze refer to the theme of intensive magnitude when dealing with the differential. To use Deleuze's terminology, intensive magnitude is "intensity."[21] Both Nishida and Deleuze, who discuss the differential, share this theory of intensive magnitude/intensity. In a sense, it is an inevitable theory for a philosophy of life that is developed under the influence of Neo-Kantianism.

Why a Discussion of Numbers?

Nishida further expands his theory of infinity in order to examine the continuity of intensive magnitude. In this connection, he frequently takes up a discussion of Cantor. Nishida's examination may be insufficient from the perspective of the foundations of mathematics. This is because, at this point, Nishida had not yet attained an understanding of the paradoxes involved in the theory of infinity. It is only in his later years, when he discusses the absolute contradic-

---

19   *NKZ*, 2: 79.
20   *NKZ*, 2: 79.
21   In French, both *intension* and *intensity* are *intensité*. In translations of Deleuze, this term is often rendered as "intensity," and his theory is thus presented as an ontology of intensity.

tory self-identity, that he faces the logic of Cantor's theory of infinity itself. Nevertheless, Nishida's references to set theory contain many interesting ideas.

An example is Nishida's discussion of "cardinal numbers" and "ordinal numbers." In his discussion of Cantor, Nishida takes up the difference between them. He describes a cardinal number as a number of the world of mere representation (that is, the determined consciousness). Cardinal numbers possess no order; they are numbers of a homogeneously depicted space. In contrast, when one deals with the infinite continuum itself—or to use Cantor's terminology, the "transfinite number" of "infinite cardinality"—ordinal numbers become significant. Here, according to Nishida, "the ideal becomes real; relations become real."[22] He describes an ordinal number as a number that deals with a qualitative (and hence, intensive) phenomenon, such as the "saturation level of red," the hue of the color red.

Here, one recalls Deleuze's distinction between the cardinal number and ordinal number in *Difference and Repetition*, where he takes up the third synthesis of time, which deals with becoming itself. Like Nishida, he presents the ordinal number as a concept that displays the temporality of intensity. The issue for both Nishida and Deleuze is, of course, the issue of infinity. In illustrating the infinitude of the ideal continuum as what is real, both of these thinkers take up the concept of number dealt with in set theory. Perhaps this was another inevitable consequence involved in a philosophy of life.

It could be objected that this is only an instance of philosophers adapting a rigorous mathematical theory to fit their own interests. However, as we have seen, Nishida and Deleuze's references to the differential calculus and set theory are not eccentric appeals. Nor are they presenting a mere analogy between philosophy and mathematics. For the use of mathematics can be said to be inevitable when dealing ontologically with the virtual infinity of the flow itself, and in disentangling the heterogeneously continuous intensive magnitude of the flow. Insofar as the philosophy of life posits the ideal totality as something given from the outset, and attempts to discern a method of depicting this as

---

22   *NKZ*, 3: 356.

something other than a flat expansion of the present, the reference to mathematics can be said to be inevitable.

This and other related issues of intensive magnitude will resurface in various forms in Nishida's discussions of absolute nothingness and the absolute contradictory self-identity, as it is one of his underlying themes. But while the discussion of the continuity of the flow develops into the issue of intensity, there is another discussion that is inserted between the two. That is the discussion of place as the foundation upon which discourse of the flow can take place.

3

THE LOGIC OF PLACE
The Multi-layered Factorialization of Relationships

The Step Towards a New Discussion

From pure experience, which was presented as the continuity of the flow, Nishida develops his theory in the direction of seeking the foundation that lies at its basis. This is the theory of place. The theory of place is treated both in *From the Acting to the Seeing* and in *The Self-Aware System of the Universal*, which develops the ideas of the former book.

The logical structure of the theory of place consists in resolving the difficulty involved in the theory of pure experience, namely, the notion of the totality as a flat expansion of the present, by extracting the alternate-dimensional foundation upon which the present is situated. It seeks to discern the foundation that lies one step beyond—a foundation in which the flowing organic network can be situated by existing there.

Let me explain two points regarding this kind of place, in connection with the theories of pure experience and self-awareness. The first is that in the theory of place, the notion of spatiality plays a central role, in contrast to the temporality of the flow. This is clear from the fact that the theory is treated in a book entitled *From the Acting to the Seeing*. There, spatiality (the "seeing") is particularly emphasized, in contrast to the action (the "acting") of the flow. The multi-faceted depth and multi-layered structure of place, as well as the inquiry into its "limit," constitute the main pillars of this theory.

The second point is that while the theory of place emphasizes spatiality, it does not merely detach itself from the motif of practice. The discussion of spatiality can be properly understood only as an attempt of a philosophy that deals with the flow to seek the infinite end of the flow itself. The focus of the discussion is still on how practice can be possible on the backdrop of infinity.

How Did the Discussion of "Place" Arise?

The theory of place is most thoroughly treated in *From the Acting to the Seeing*. The essay at the beginning of the work, "That Which is Immediately Given," plays the role of linking Nishida's idea of self-awareness to the theory of place. What one should first notice is that, here Nishida does not conceive of the world that is immediately given in terms of sensations or perception, as he did in *An Inquiry Into the Good*: "what is immediately given is not something like a world of perception; rather it is a world of intuition, something like what an artist sees";[1] "what is immediately given is not something like sensations or perceptions ...."[2] As I have repeatedly pointed out, the problem confronting the theory of pure experience is that it cannot depict the reality of the infinitely broad flow except as an expansion of the present. This amounts to depicting the reality of the flow using sensations and perceptions as a kind of model. But when thinking of the infinity of the flow and its limit, and if one supposes that the limit is given all at once where experience is taking place, then the infinity of the flow must be depicted as something of a different dimension than the present. The infinity is not something that can be situated in the domain of the determined and actualized, such as sensations and perceptions, but must be grasped as a virtual being that cannot be fully actualized, like the dx in relation to x in the theory of self-awareness. How, then, can we approach this kind of being?

Nishida calls this flow itself, which is immediately given, but cannot be grasped as something present, the "supra-cognitive world"[3] or "supra-conscious world."[4] Consciousness—that is, sensations and perceptions situated at the level of consciousness—can be discerned only through the determination of the infinite flow from a certain

---

1   *NKZ*, 3: 268.
2   *NKZ*, 3: 273.
3   *NKZ*, 3: 270.
4   *NKZ*, 3: 272.

perspective or standpoint. But the flow itself cannot be grasped by this determination; it can only be grasped as something that envelops whatever is determined, and exists as the latter's foundation. It is, therefore, something immediately given that transcends consciousness. This kind of discussion displays an archetypical notion of place that tries to establish something that is essentially differentiated from consciousness and whatever is actualized, something that envelops these as their foundation.

However, this "supra-consciousness" is obviously related to the dynamic flow itself. This theory of the supra-conscious is treated from the standpoint of the issue of action: "whenever we assume the position of an acting subject or acting self, we are already making the supra-conscious world our object. And what is truly given as the actual is none other than what is given to this acting self."[5] This links with the theory of place.

The idea that that which "envelops" consciousness—the infinite flow—is something real and immediately given as something different from what is actualized, in turn directly connects with the discussion of temporality. Here, Nishida describes the unobjectifiable time as the "true time."[6] He thus explicates an aspect of time that he calls the "supra-temporal consciousness,"[7] which is different from the actualized present. This aspect is no longer depicted as a flat expansion of the present. Rather, what is at issue at this stage is time as "something eternal,"[8] something that includes within itself memory (past) and hope (future). That is, Nishida is discerning a time that forms a foundation, a "deep basis of reality" from which past, present, and future can be surveyed all at once. It is a time that depicts the totality of the flow of time, and lies at the basis of the present in which actions are performed. The supra-temporal consciousness, as something that constitutes a totality, is linked with the phrase "eternity."

Here I want to show that this discussion is deeply related to Bergson's notion of pure memory, in the way that it deals with the supra-temporal.

---

5   *NKZ*, 3: 272.
6   *NKZ*, 3: 275.
7   *NKZ*, 3: 274.
8   *NKZ*, 3: 276.

The Supra-Temporal

Bergson develops his theory of pure memory mostly in his second book, *Matter and Memory*. This theory builds on his theory of time that he discussed previously in *An Essay on the Immediate Data of Consciousness*, which, like Nishida's *An Inquiry into the Good*, had relied upon the notions of perception and sensation.

Recall that pure duration is an indivisible flow. Thus, as I mentioned in connection with the model of the mirror in the theory of self-awareness, if one grants the reality of pure duration, then one is led to a rather peculiar vision in which the past is prioritized over the actualized present. In principle, all that is past is connected with the present. The present can only be depicted as the tip of the vast flow of the past. Thus, if one assumes that the flow itself is real, it follows that what is real in an even stronger sense is not the present, which is a mere cross section of the flow, but the past that forms the virtuality of the flow.

Thus, for Bergson, it is the totality of the past that is real. The past is depicted as a vast series of strata that envelop the present, which is nothing but a cross section. Bergson calls this past, this virtual totality, "pure memory." And he posits this pure memory behind the present, as something that possesses a "difference in nature" from the actualized present because it is virtual.

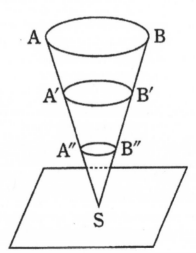

Bergson illustrates the totality of pure memory using the model of the cone of memory. The cone is a model that displays the reality of memory itself. Pure memory is the totality of the cone, whose base is open. The various strata of the cone correspond to the flows in which the present is in the process of moving and repeating, in accordance with their own degree of generality, the totality of memory. In the figure above, as one approaches the tip of the cone (the present), the degree of generality increases, and as one approaches the base of the cone, the degree of particularity increases. Here, the concretized memory (the "memory-image" as representation) is extracted through determination of the totality of pure memory. This is none other than the differenciation of a virtual flow into something concrete. But the infinity of pure memory is a site of the force of the totality itself, which cannot be grasped by differenciation.

This links with Nishida's notion of a supra-consciousness beyond consciousness and with his idea of positing the "true time" as a supra-temporal consciousness that cannot be discerned in actuality. Like Bergson, Nishida regards the infinite force that lies behind the determined actualities as a place. This is described as a time that displays the supra-temporal consciousness, a time that cannot be resolved into a present-centered time.

Let me explain the supra-temporal in a bit more detail. Positing a domain of pure memory that is different from the present leads to a further paradoxical consequence. The existence of the totality of the past, pure memory is no longer depicted from the standpoint of a temporal axis centered on the present. That is, everything that is past is depicted as existing simultaneously, without a fixed reference point called the present. The past is regarded as existing simultaneously with itself and with the present; in other words, the past, as something that exists simultaneously, constitutes the various strata of memory.

This is linked with the way in which Nishida brings together the temporal dimensions of past, present, and future in the supra-temporal consciousness via the "infinitely deep" contained within the present.[9] This simultaneous conception of time is not based on the

---

9   *NKZ*, 3: 275.

domain of the actualized, such as perception and sensation; it does not make the actual the foundation of the temporal series. Rather, it is inevitably involved in any attempt to release the totality of the flow that is assumed to lie behind the actual, without positing a fixed point. To use Deleuze's terminology, Nishida is adopting a "surveying" viewpoint of "infinite velocity" upon the flow. To intuit the virtual totality by surveying is to extract the situation peculiar to a time that grasps the flow, without positing a center called the present.

The Factorialization of Relationships

In an essay entitled "Place," Nishida formulates reality as the supra-consciousness that was sketched in "That Which is Immediately Given." He thus presents the concept of place. What is important here is that a system called the *factorialization of relationships* is introduced in the concept of place. Nishida's discussion, which steps directly into the infinite flow, is able to avoid the dead end of treating the totality of relationships as an expansion of the present by factorializing the relationships.

The essay "Place" (1926) begins with a discussion of systems and that which maintains them: "in order to say that two objects are mutually related and form a single system that maintains itself, we must think of that which maintains this system, and of that within which the system can exist and function. Whatever *is* must be *within* someplace."[10] Pure experience is itself a system. It is a flow, a relationship. But in order to say that there exists ("is") a relationship, there must be something like a foundation within which the relationship itself is enveloped. There must be a place that envelops the relationship.

This is what Nishida calls "place." It is formulated by the expression "to be within." For example, let us think of an object existing in space. Space can be said to be nothing but a relationship between two objects. The relation and the *relata* (the objects) are one. This is how we discern physical space. This is a "pure-experiential" development that

---

contemplates a system of relations. However, this physical space, as a relation, must itself be related to a different physical space. There must be something other than the relation that is physical space. Thus, there must be a place *within* which the physical space can exist (3–416). In other words, there must be a relationship for the relationship.

We can also think of conscious phenomena, the field of consciousness, and an object: "whenever we think of something, there must be a place where this something is projected. We can first think of this place as a field of consciousness."[11] The phenomena of consciousness first arise in this kind of field of consciousness. Conscious phenomena, as something continuous, are mutual relationships. These conscious phenomena, as relationships, first exist in a field of consciousness. However, we must also think of the object (of consciousness). The object is grasped as something independent of consciousness. Then what happens? There must then be something that "envelops" both the object and consciousness so that they can be brought into relation.[12] That is, in the place ("field of consciousness") where events arise as relationships, there must be a further place within which something else (the object) is related.

This logic of the factorialization of relationships is applicable to any situation that involves relationships. In order to explain an event that is a relationship, a place wherein this event can exist is assumed over and over again. This is not something that can be depicted by a flat expansion of relationships, as in the theory of pure experience. What is significant here is the factorialization of relationships, the fact that the experience of a relationship is "within" someplace.

The Place "Within" Which the Color Red Is

Taking the example of color, Nishida argues as follows.[13] Red is a color, but non-red things are also colors. The place "within" which the color red is must be a place "within" which red is, and also "within" a place of non-red. Thus, as something that contains both

---

11   *NKZ*, 3: 416.
12   *NKZ*, 3: 417.
13   *NKZ*, 3:442–44.

being and non-being, it must be something that is not a color. This kind of "place within which something is" is in the first place a thing. But for a philosophy that grasps events as systems, things are melted together into relations. Thus, that which contains both the being and non-being of red must be a single act rather than a thing. Yet this act, which encompasses relations, must contain a virtual being. And, furthermore, this virtual being must involve a place.

At the basis of this kind of single act that contains within itself both being and non-being, that is, both change and its opposite (such as red and non-red), one must posit a single genus concept (in the case of red, *color* would be the genus concept). Change is opposition within a genus concept (such as the concept of color). The virtual being in a genus concept is a being thought in the opposition between being and non-being (such as red and non-red). But the place where this kind of opposition occurs is not yet the "true place." The true place should not be understood in terms of an opposition between being and non-being. It must be outside of the genus concept. Thus, Nishida writes that there must be a place of "arising and ceasing" rather than a place of "change." Only then can nothingness appear, not as something opposed to being, but as something that transcends the opposition between being and non-being, something within which both can arise. There must be a "place of nothingness" that is not opposed to being, but envelops such an opposition.

In this way, Nishida argues for a factorialization of relations. That is, starting from the opposition between the "being" of a relationship and its "non-being," he posits a "virtual being" that contains this opposition, and furthermore a "true place of nothingness" that contains this virtual being; the discussion of relationships thus leads to a situation of nothingness. In this nothingness, one surpasses "the acting" and is led to "the seeing." This discussion is a typical development of factorialization.

However, instead of going immediately into the nothingness to which the discussion of place leads, let us first examine the structure of place in a bit more detail. The discussion of nothingness (as well as the discussion of the absolute nothingness that lies a further step beyond nothingness) will be presented immediately afterwards.

Predicate Logic

The theory of place is discerned by developing the theory of self-awareness towards the basis that supports it. A place is something within which something exists, a place within which something is— something that lies behind that which is objectified as consciousness, something that envelops. And by its very nature, this place is something that is repeatedly factualized, depicting an even deeper place that contains everything. How can we illustrate the structure of this place? And by what kind of multi-layered character can we organize and grasp this structure?

Nishida's multi-layered discussion of place is deepened in the path of development in *From the Acting to the Seeing* to *The Self-Aware System of the Universal*. Here, following the logic of place, he extracts the "universal of judgment" (the judgment of the natural world), the "self-aware universal" (consciousness), and the "intelligible world" ("intellectual intuition"),[14] and reaches the bottomless place of absolute nothingness, which encompasses the intelligible world. The sketch of place is thus complete.

Now, what should we discuss when thinking of the multi-stratified structure of place? We should discuss the predicate logic, which is a logical structure peculiar to Nishida. What, then, is predicate logic? What we first ought to realize is that predicate logic is not subject logic. Subject logic is the idea that there is a pre-determined subject that constitutes the center of a judgment. It is the idea that judgments such as "I am ..." or "I do ..." are understood by being contained within the subject called the "I." Nishida describes this kind of subject as an "individual that is a subject but never a predicate."[15] He calls this individual-based logic "Aristotelian logic."[16]

For Nishida, this kind of individual is not what is meant when we say that "I am."[17] The individual called the "I" is something particular. It can only be thought as something "within" a universal that envelops this particularity. In other words, the individual called the "I,"

---

14   *NKZ*, 4: 101.
15   *NKZ*, 4: 15.
16   *NKZ*, 4: 284.
17   *NKZ*, 4: 15.

which is something actualized, can only be thought as being rooted in the place of a universal where such individuals exist. This place of universals appears as a "predicate aspect," as opposed to the subject. Rather than positing the subject as something pre-determined, we must suppose that there is a "predicate aspect" prior to the subject called the "I," and this predicate aspect is something that gains meaning only through the subject that exists within it. Nishida describes this circumstance as follows:

> The I is not the unification of a grammatical subject. It is a predicative unification. It is not a point but a circle. It is not a thing but a place.[18]

> While the I is individual, it is not individual in the sense of being the subject of a proposition. Whatever is singular is its own predicate, and whatever is its own predicate is merely self-identical. But when the predicate aspect of something self-identical is thought to envelop something subjective within itself, that is, when the subject is thought to be immersed in the predicate, it is thought that I am. The copula "am" signifies on the one hand that the particular is within the universal, and on the other hand it signifies the self-determination of the universal.[19]

A place is not the place of the subject. The center of a subjective judgment is discerned only through the determination of such a place. In this sense, the individual called the "I," which is particular, must first become "immersed" in the universal predicate aspect. And at the same time, concrete judgments are formed through the self-determination of the predicate aspect. The categories and concepts that form judgments are also extracted from this self-determination of place. Let us look at Nishida's passages once more:

> The subjective is within the predicate aspect, and the two are fused together in a judgment. The subjective determination of the predicate aspect becomes the judgment. The forms of the subjective determination of the predicate aspect itself are the so-called categories, and these give rise to various kinds of judgment.[20]

---

18   *NKZ*, 3: 469.
19   *NKZ*, 4: 15.
20   *NKZ*, 4: 26.

> In order for a concept to become truly concrete and have an object within itself, that is, in order for conceptual knowledge to ground itself through itself, there must be a place, a direct determination of a universal.[21]

Regarding this kind of predicate logic, which holds that "the so-called relation of subsumption, where the subject is contained within the predicate, is the fundamental significance of a judgment,"[22] Yujirō Nakamura has made an interesting claim.[23] He points out that there is a similarity between Nishida's discussion and so-called "paleo-logic," and furthermore, citing the accounts of psychiatrists such as Kimura Bin, he explicates the overlap between this and the "schizophrenic" way of using language.

Normally, our language is subjective. But in paleo-logical or schiz-ophrenic discourses, there is a peculiar move of the subject to the predicate, as in "I am A"; "Some other person B is A"; "therefore, I am some other person B." This does not merely indicate a deviation from the ordinary use of language. Rather, it illustrates the structure of a deep stratum of life itself, a stratum that lies below the superficial language where the world of Aristotelian logic is situated.

The Predicate Aspect and the Universal

In order to consider Nishida's discussion properly, let us take a look at how this corresponds to Bergson's discussion. From the standpoint of the philosophy of life, what Nishida is trying to say in his predicate logic is clearly related to Bergson's development of the theory of pure memory in the direction of the universal concept. Bergson uses the conical model of memory not only as something that indicates the existence of memory itself, but also as a model that describes the nature of universal concepts (see chapter three of *Matter and Memory*).

As I have already mentioned, Bergson's theory of the reality of the flow regards all that is past as a virtual reality. And like Nishida, in order

---

21 *NKZ*, 4: 52.
22 *NKZ*, 4: 50.
23 Nakamura Yujirō, *Nishida Kitarō 1* (Tokyo: Iwanami, 2001).

to posit the present, he had to describe the determination of something from the vast reality of the past, illustrated by the cone. Let us here consider concepts and judgments. From the above perspective, pure memory is the accumulation of an infinitely connected past, upon which concepts and judgments rely. And the various strata of memory, illustrated by the cone, each display their own degree of generality and individuality (as I have already explained, the degree of generality increases as one approaches the tip of the cone, and the degree of individuality increases as one approaches the basis of the cone).

Thus, the various strata of memory are described as universal concepts of varying degrees of generality. And a judgment is an act of going through these strata of universal concepts and actualizing one that applies to a certain situation. In such a situation, a certain concept that lies between the tip and base of the cone (and hence with some degree of generality and some degree of individuality) is discerned in accordance with the situation. Thus, by separating a concept from the totality of memory and unfolding it in the present situation, a concrete judgment is made.

It is evident that this discussion overlaps with the essence of Nishida's predicate logic and his theory of place. Bergson's theory describes how a concept and judgment arise in the present as a determination of a universal concept, which is depicted as the past. In the case of Nishida, the universal is regarded as the predicate aspect. Yet what both of these thinkers describe is an act of conceptualization that is rooted in the multi-layered depths of a reality that is depicted intensively. It is an actualization in the light of an infinite background. Bergson describes this in terms of the universal concept, while Nishida describes this in terms of the predicate aspect.

Predicate logic itself is something that is displayed in the most superficial part of the theory of place, namely, the theory of judgment; that is, it is displayed in the realm closest to the objectified realm. It can be said to describe the structure that makes possible the linguistically articulated domain that is treated by concepts. However, Nishida will continue to use the term universal to refer to the multiple strata of place. This indicates that predicate logic is able to capture the structure that runs through the totality of the theory of place.

What Is the Intelligible World?

Next let us examine how Nishida depicts the multi-layered character of place. His essays, "The Intelligible World" and "The Self-determination of the Universal," published in *The Self-Aware System of the Universal* (1930), will be helpful in this connection. As I have already mentioned, Nishida describes place as something that has a fundamentally factorial structure, in the sense that any place within which something is itself requires a place within which it is.

The predicate logic developed in the theory of judgment accurately expresses the nature of Nishida's theory, which does not rely on the subject. But the level of conceptualization that becomes an issue in the theory of judgment is a superficial issue in his theory of place. It is thus re-oriented in a more thorough manner in the direction of the "acting," that is, as being the flow itself.

The judgmental universal wherein the judgment is situated is first enveloped in the self-aware universal, which is the stage of consciousness. And the self-aware universal is further situated in what is called the "intelligible world." And finally, the intelligible world is depicted as being "within" what is called "absolute nothingness." This is the result of Nishida's radically thinking through the idea that the flow is continuous, and that there is a base to the world of acting wherein the flow itself is generated:

> The enveloping of the judgmental universal within the self-aware universal gives rise to intellectual intuition, and furthermore, the enveloping of the self-aware universal within the universal of intellectual intuition causes the conscious self to go beyond itself and become the intelligible self.[24]

> Thus, even the universal of intellectual intuition [the intelligible world] is not yet last. There must still be a universal, something like a place of Absolute Nothingness that envelops this.[25]

In this way, Nishida presents, in its multi-layered character, the nature of place as a self-aware system of the universal. Let us first dis-

---

24 *NKZ*, 4: 117.
25 *NKZ*, 4: 142.

cuss the intelligible world and then absolute nothingness, so that we can consider the significance of this multi-layered character.

What is the intelligible world? It is a site of intellectual intuition or "seeing" rooted in the flow itself, "within" which lies the consciousness that supports the "judgmental aspect." It can be said to be a world of seeing from which the infinity of the flow itself and all the acts that take place there can be surveyed. At this stage, acting is depicted as overlapping with seeing. Nishida explains this intuition of the flow by citing the artist's creative act as an example: "only when one has reached something like the artistic intuition can one determine something that is truly within the universal of intellectual intuition, that is, something that intuits its own content. Here, to act is to see";[26] "intellectual intuition is the self's act of truly seeing itself, of seeing its own depths."[27]

How should we think about this intellectual intuition, this act of "seeing"? How should we grasp this situation that is like the act of seeing at the bottom of action, a situation that gives the impression of the suspension of motion?

The Paradox of Seeing Without a Fixed Point

In a sense, this situation is the act of seeing the continuity of the infinite flow itself. Intellectual intuition is none other than the act of "seeing" the infinity of this movement. In the case of a judging self, something close to the surface is posited—a central subject, a fixed point of the flow called the present. However, at the stage of intellectual intuition, one faces the paradoxical task of making sense of the act of seeing the infinite flow without any fixed point.

Using Bergson's conical model, we can say that intellectual intuition is a state where the various strata of memory appear as they are, without the tip of the cone. As I mentioned earlier, one could imagine a situation where memory is released as it is, without a temporal axis.

---

26   *NKZ*, 4: 128.
27   *NKZ*, 4: 129.

To use Deleuze's terminology again, one could say that intellectual intuition is the act of "surveying" the flow with "infinite velocity."

To "survey" and grasp the entire flow—this is the act of intellectual intuition, of seeing the movement. It is the act of seeing the world, the infinite totality of movements within movements, as (virtual) invisible forces that cannot be grasped as individual objects. Thus, although it is described in visual terms, it is a special kind of seeing that cannot be understood in terms of ordinary vision—it is, as it were, the act of seeing the infinite.

This does not mean, however, that the intelligible world implies a suspension of motion. By no means does it signify the attainment of a state unrelated to action. This can be understood from the fact that Nishida describes the intelligible world as a world of "expression": "it is in the expressive consciousness that we can say we have attained the position of the intelligible self. The intelligible self determines itself expressively. What is thought of as expressive consciousness possesses the significance of intelligible consciousness."[28]

"Expression" is the presentation of the force of infinity. To "express" is to give form to the infinite itself while bearing the infinite flow. Thus, the intelligible world, insofar as it is the basis of action, is deeply related to the fact that to act is to create something. The artist is capable of creativity only by virtue of the circumstance that through her creative act, she sees the infinite depth in an instant. The concept of the intelligible world describes this same circumstance.

In his essay, "The Self-Aware Determination of the Universal," Nishida inserts an account of historical acts between his discussions of the intelligible world and absolute nothingness.[29] He also calls this the "acting self" and reconceives the intelligible universal as an "acting universal" in the narrow sense.[30] In the latter half of this essay, Nishida re-conceptualizes the intelligible world in terms of the "expressive universal" and the "acting universal." This shows that the intelligible world is related to the themes of action and creation in action.

---

28   *NKZ*, 4: 295.
29   *NKZ*, 4: 313.
30   *NKZ*, 4: 358.

The Transcendent Necessary for the Beyond

The other issue at stake in our discussion is how Nishida further develops his concept of the absolute nothingness that is posited beyond the intelligible world. He writes: "that which envelops the universal of intellectual intuition—that within which our true self is thought to be—is something that ought to be called a place of absolute nothingness. This ought to be thought of as a religious consciousness."[31]

The notion of absolute nothingness is a radicalization of the theory of place. The intelligible world is a place where one sees the infinite itself. Therefore, it can also be depicted as a place where one sees the nothingness of the world perceived as an object (the world where being and non-being are opposed), the nothingness that envelops both being and non-being. The act of seeing the invisible infinity—an infinity that cannot be objectified—is what the intelligible world consists in. However, insofar as the intelligible world, though related to nothingness, is a world of expression that makes action possible, it is something that "possesses a relation with conceptual knowledge."[32] Therefore, it is still related to consciousness and being. It follows, Nishida argues, that we must suppose "a world of mystic intuition that defies language and thought,"[33] a world that goes beyond the above way of apprehending the infinite—the world of absolute nothingness. This is a place that no longer has any relation to being, a place where "not only is there no longer a self that sees; there is no longer any idea to be seen."[34] Nishida describes this as a world of "deep internal life."[35]

Insofar as place is depicted as a multi-layered factorialization of relationships, one cannot avoid positing a kind of limit of the factorialization. Since the intelligible world is the grasping of the infinity of the flow itself, it is in a sense a limit. But given that this is depicted as an act of seeing the totality of the flow, it is possible to posit further below a

---

31   *NKZ*, 4: 145.
32   *NKZ*, 4: 145.
33   *NKZ*, 4: 145.
34   *NKZ*, 4: 324.
35   *NKZ*, 4: 325.

place "within" which the totality of the flow itself is, a place that is no longer a place. This is the place of absolute nothingness.

Conceptually, absolute nothingness is a "nothing" that is discerned outside of the infinity of the flow. If the intelligible world is a world of expression where one sees what cannot be seen, absolute nothingness is an infinite "beyond" that is postulated as something that envelops this intelligible world. In other words, it is a "transcendent" that is necessary to stop the progression of the factorialization of place.

Insofar as the discussion of the totality of the infinity of the flow is a discussion of a totality, it is inevitable that Nishida developed a concept of transcendence that governs this totality, even if the totality is depicted in terms of factorialization (rather than a flat expansion of the present). And it is also inevitable that this concept of transcendence is depicted as "nothingness," something that cannot be spoken of. But, if, like Nishida, one posits this nothingness as a kind of religious state, then one is falling into the same problem that Nishida himself fell into in *An Inquiry Into the Good*, albeit in a plane different from actualization—namely, one is trapped in the dead-end of depicting the totality as a substantive entity, even if it is called "nothingness."

Nishida's discussion of absolute nothingness was subject to a very reasonable and sharp criticism by his student Tanabe Hajime. And Nishida, in response to Tanabe's critique, went on to modify his theory of nothingness. This does not mean that he succumbed to Tanabe's critique. Rather, in light of Tanabe's critique, he reconnected nothingness, the limit of intensive magnitude, with the theme of action.

"Place" as a Theory of Life

It was evident to both Nishida and Bergson that the theory of pure experience or pure duration could be construed as a naïve expansion of a psychological account, and that is was not enough to depict the infinity of relationships. In like manner, they both tried to go beyond the logic of relationships that employs a vaguely defined notion of totality. It was in the endeavor to attain a way of speaking about life that went beyond the idea of the organic that the theory of place and logic of environment were introduced.

The structure of this logic should be evident by now. It consists of topologically factorializing the relationships of life characterized as organic, and presenting that which envelops these relationships as a different (foundational) relationship. In contrast to relationships, what is at issue here is factorialization, the relationship of relationships. Through the presentation of a different phase, the dead-end of the organic totality takes on a double (or multi-layered) perspective; and by showing the difference in strata, the difficulty apparently seems to be resolved.

There are many theories of life that make "environment" a keyword. The existence of life is situated in a place or environment. Therefore, if one considers the unique function of life, one realizes that life is deeply shaped by place and environment. It is well-known that organisms are able to swiftly change the color of their body in one day or night according to the place that they are at, or easily change their form according to differences in place (e.g., the differences regarding which tributary of a river the organism is in, and differences of minute components in the water). It is also probably well-known that insects and fish are able to change their developmental form, or even their sex, depending on the density of the swarm or the school that they are a part of; and the density and nature of the swarm or school are in turn shaped by the broader environment and climate in which they are embedded. Again, as displayed by the example of the carabid beetle, individuals with similar DNA compositions express different forms if they are placed in very different environments. They manifest colors and forms that are very similar to other individuals in the same environment, even if those other individuals have a different kind of DNA composition.

In this sense, it is a natural idea that life's unique plasticity and diverse manners of reception should be explained, not in terms of the relationships that life itself possesses (that is, the internal environment of the individual such as genes and traits), but in terms of the diversity of the environments that encompass these relationships. Now, what is the logic that describes this kind of place or environment? It is a logic that extracts that which envelops relationships as an alternate kind of relationship with a phase difference, that is, as a relationship of relationships. In contrast to the internal environment (which is a single relationship), such as genes and traits, this logic presents an alternate relationship, such as the external environment that encompasses the internal environment, and thereby establishes a relationship of relationships. It can be said to be a logic that seeks in an alternate phase the foundation of relationships, although this foundation is something that is itself a relationship.

Theoretically speaking, this project corresponds to Bergson's theory of pure memory. The path of development that Bergson's thought took, from duration to memory, overlaps with the path that Nishida took, deepening the theory of pure experience, and ultimately reaching the theory of place and absolute nothingness.

At the Limit of the Factorialization of Relationships

Bergson illustrates pure memory as the past that repeats itself infinitely by using the conical model of memory. Here, duration (relationship) is not described as a mere expansion of the present. Pure memory is depicted as something that possesses a "difference in nature" from the present, as the various strata of a cone that contains the present as its tip. Pure memory is presented as a vast and multi-layered reality that encompasses and envelops the present (and its organic relationships).

This description of memory bears a strong structural resemblance to Nishida's theory of place. This is because Nishida's theory of place is a theory that shows that the individual, while embedded in a network of relationships, is ultimately "within" an alternate-dimensional relationship that encompasses these relationships. The theory of place illustrates how the relationships themselves are one by one subsumed under a different relationship in a multi-layered fashion. It is clear that this theory resolves the difficulties associated with organic holism and is furthermore an attempt to ground it.

As I have already mentioned, organic holism is an idea that hypostatizes the infinite breadth of relationships and conceives of the individual from the side of the totality. It is based on the expansion of the present. But in the theories of pure memory and place, which posit a different level that subsumes the present, the centrality of the present is dismantled and the phase of the discussion is shifted. The flatness of organic holism's expansion of the present is thereby avoided.

These logics are based on a relationship that encompasses relationships. However, if we apply the logic of factorialization that posits a relationship of relationships, the movement of factorialization will be unstoppable and go on *ad infinitum* (the relationship of relationships of relationships and so on). If we stop the movement somewhere, the totality is again hypostatized and we end up with the same result as holism. If we posit place as an external environment that envelops the internal environment, then there must in turn be an environment that envelops this external environment and this movement will be limitless, both spatially and temporally. If we posit a limit somewhere, then that limit will be the foundation that plays the role of the totality; here, we end up with the same logic as holism. Thus, just as the infinite expansion of relationships resulted in a dead-end, this kind of factorialization faces the difficulty that it cannot continue indefinitely.

How could one deal with this difficulty? The only solution seems to be to depict the "limit" that envelops everything else as being transcendent, which then possess a kind of absolute phase difference. As we saw earlier, Nishida's logic of place ultimately leads to absolute nothingness. This can be understood as a kind of transcendent, bottomless bottom that results from inquisition into the relationship of relationships. However, does not the characterization of absolute nothingness as being transcendent amount to evading the totality of holism by means of factorialization, and then positing its ultimate foundation as an impredicable something, that is, as "nothing"? What is this "something"? If this question is pressed, are we not forced to re-examine the logic of place? Does not this theory fall into the trap involving the notion of an impredicable thing called "nothingness," as pointed out in Tanabe Hajime's critique (which we will see in the following chapter)?

The logic of Nishida characterized by the concepts of acting intuition and the absolute contradictory self-identity is, I believe, the result of such re-examination. This logic expresses the final form of

Nishida's thought. It can also be understood as the final form of the philosophy of life. But before we go into this, we must investigate Nishida's structural transformation of the state of nothingness. This will lead us directly to the late Nishida's theory.

4

THE DEVELOPMENT OF
ABSOLUTE NOTHINGNESS
The Theoretical Introduction of Discontinuity

Tanabe Hajime's Critique of Nishida

There are many things to talk about when it comes to the relation between Tanabe Hajime (1885–1962) and Nishida. To all appearances, Tanabe was Nishida's legitimate successor. That was his position in academia. It was Nishida who discovered Tanabe and invited him to Kyoto University. And among Nishida's dazzling students of the Kyoto School, Tanabe was someone who could rival Nishida in terms of having developed an original philosophy (the "Logic of Species"). However, Tanabe expressed an attitude towards Nishida that any student faced with a mentor who adamantly advocates a highly original philosophy must necessarily express. Tanabe was Nishida's sharpest critic.

The complex relationship between the two men can be discussed from various angles, including their emotional interrelation. Eventually they will drift apart, making less and less personal contact. Yet, when one takes a look at Tanabe's first critique of Nishida, "Request for Professor Nishida's Guidance,"[1] one realizes that Tanabe's criticism, far from being emotional, is a very reasonable one.

First, Tanabe's criticism accurately points out the difficulties in Nishida's theory. It succeeds in laying bare the issue for Nishida. Second, there is Nishida's response to the criticism. Nishida attempted to develop his theory in light of Tanabe's critique. However, this does not mean that he followed Tanabe's opinion. While giving due considera-

---

1   Printed in *Tanabe Hajime Zenshū* (Complete Works of Hajime Tanabe), Vol. 4 (Tokyo: Chikuma, 1963), here after *THZ*. Hereinafter, all citations of Tanabe will be from this volume; page numbers will be indicated in parentheses.

tion to Tanabe's critique, he nonetheless emphasizes his own philosophical attitude in a way different from Tanabe. In this sense, one can
say that Tanabe's critique possessed the power to clarify what the issue
was, and to highlight the differences between the two men.

What is it, then, that Tanabe criticized in Nishida? The answer
is simple. He criticized Nishida's concept of absolute nothingness.
He points out that Nishida's theory, while starting from a noetic
standpoint,[2] is itself a kind of Plotinism, according to which everything "emanates" hierarchically from an ineffable "one."[3] And he goes
on to suggest that this is no longer a "philosophical" theory. Let us
look at the criticism in more detail.

Retracing Nishida's factorial construction of the theory of place,
Tanabe does not fail to praise the originality of Nishida's work, especially with respect to predicate logic, remarking that, in a sense, it
continues and goes beyond the developments of German Idealism.
However, at the point where Nishida's theory goes beyond the self-
awareness of the intelligible self and reaches the absolute nothingness
that lies on the other side, Tanabe's appraisal becomes harsher. He
writes as follows:

> This deep doctrine which teaches that self-love is self-existence, by the reason
> that to return to the true self that sees oneself in nothingness is to love oneself, is
> a confession of Professor Nishida's unique experience, and all I can do is express
> by veneration for such rare and profound thought. However, is it possible to
> systematize this kind of religious experience in the form of a philosophy?[4]

> I do not intend to ignore the characteristic of the self-awareness of nothingness
> that Prof. Nishida propounds in lieu of the self-awareness of being. Nonetheless,
> it seems inevitable to me that by the self-awareness of absolute nothingness, the
> universals at every stage, as well as the places within which those universals are,
> will be noetically transformed into the self, and furthermore, that everything will

---

2   *Noetic* is originally a term used in Husserl's phenomenology to describe the struc-
    ture of consciousness. The term is used in contrast with the expression *noematic*,
    which describes the act of relating with objects in consciousness through their
    meaning. The *noetic* is thus the aspect of consciousness linked with acts that con-
    stitute such objects. In other words, the *noematic* is the aspect of the object grasped
    by consciousness, while the *noetic* is the aspect of the act of consciousness that con-
    stitutes these objects.

3   *THZ*, 4: 300.

4   *THZ*, 4: 307.

become a shadow, enveloped in the light of calm contemplation and resignation, so that raw reality and action will completely lose their original meaning.[5]

Tanabe criticizes Nishida's concept of absolute nothingness, suggesting that it is merely an expression of his unique "religious experience." That is, he is questioning whether such a religious self-awareness can be systematized in the form of a philosophy. Tanabe is thus criticizing Nishida's approach itself.

According to Tanabe, while Nishida's theory of place seeks a noetic limit (a limit of action), its positing of absolute nothingness at the limit ultimately defeats the purpose of the theory, which is to root consciousness in the flow (the "raw reality") and action. In other words, Tanabe is suggesting that the concept of absolute nothingness annuls the dynamic movement of action.

From Which Side Should We Speak?

Of course, Tanabe fully understands that, when Nishida speaks of absolute nothingness, he is postulating a limit of the flow (that is, the "acting") so as to procure a place for its infinitude. This is apparent from Tanabe's following remarks: "in other words, religious experience is supra-historical, while philosophical reflection is relative to history. From the outset, the historical is founded on the supra-historical, and the relative anticipates the absolute."[6] He continues: "the supra-historical that is anticipated as the basis of the historical is simply the differential contained within the historical; it is none other than an *Idee* that can be infinitely sought in the latter."[7] Thus, for Tanabe as well as for Nishida, assuming a domain of the "*Idee*" (idea) overlaps with the notion of absolute nothingness. This goes in the same direction as Nishida, in that it conceives of the totality of the flow (and its limit) as an "idea." However, Nishida regarded this idea as something that is "immediately given." The absolute nothingness can be said to be the limit of an idea that is immediately given.

---

5   *THZ*, 4: 302.
6   *THZ*, 4: 311.
7   *THZ*, 4: 311.

For Tanabe, on the other hand, the idea is merely anticipated as something that is infinitely sought. Hence, the supra-historical, which is an idea that can only be anticipated, can be spoken of only from the side of relative history. The issue between the two men is, therefore, the issue of from which side to speak.

According to Tanabe, who starts his discussion form the side of the historical, Nishida's approach of positing the supra-historical idea in its immediacy is tantamount to Plotinus's theory of emanation, according to which everything emanates stepwise from the one. Hence his criticism: "if philosophy were to posit an ultimate, ineffable universal, and interpret actual existence as a self-determination of this universal, would this not lead to an abandonment of philosophy?"[8]

Furthermore, later in the same essay, Tanabe again criticizes Nishida's criticism of phenomenology and Kant's philosophy. The same framework can be discerned here as well. According to Nishida, Husserl's theory rests content at the stage of intentional consciousness and does not reach the "intellectual self-awareness of the internal life" that envelops this consciousness.[9] And while Kant's philosophy may have reached Nishida's stage of the intelligible, from the standpoint of absolute nothingness, it is a theory that draws attention to the "historically conditioned" nature of "consciousness in general."[10]

Let us put aside the issue here of whether or not Nishida's dogmatic judgment of other philosophers is defensible. What we should notice is that Tanabe criticizes Nishida again. According to Tanabe, it is true that Husserl has not reached the depths of self-awareness (here, Tanabe has in mind Husserl's middle period of transcendental idealism). Nonetheless, insofar as Husserl advocates phenomenology as an "exact science," it is inevitable that he should have "rested content with contemplating the essence of intentional consciousness."[11] Furthermore, "the intelligible universal that sees the Idea, or its intellectual aspect—consciousness in general—is relative to history, and

---

8   *THZ*, 4: 309.
9   *THZ*, 4: 321.
10   *THZ*, 4: 326.
11   *THZ*, 4: 321.

cannot escape being conditioned by it."[12] Philosophy thus has no choice but to speak from the side of the "historically conditioned"; therefore, Nishida's criticism of Husserl and Kant are off the mark; thus runs Tanabe's criticism.

Again, the key issue here is which side to speak from. Tanabe's point is that philosophy cannot start its discourse from the immediacy of absolute nothingness, which Nishida situates at the basis of his inquiry.

Re-Depicting Absolute Nothingness

How did Nishida react to Tanabe's criticism? How can we understand the significance of the criticism? Nishida did not fail to respond to Tanabe's critique. This is apparent from the fact that in his *Self-Aware Determination of Nothingness*, which I will discuss next, Nishida shifts the discussion towards the direction of action itself, with Tanabe's critique in mind.

However, the way Nishida responds to Tanabe's critique is subtle. He does not abandon his notion of absolute nothingness as the limit of place. His insistence that we must discuss the self-aware determination of nothingness seems to be a complete rejection of Tanabe's critique. Even if absolute nothingness were a kind of religious state, it is necessary insofar as the infinite is given immediately in what Nishida considers to be "acting" reality. Inasmuch as our life—this life of intensive continuity—touches the infinite, there must be a nothingness contained within the actions of this life.

Yet at the same time, Nishida clearly shifts the discussion of absolute nothingness. In one respect, this is probably because Tanabe's critique accurately pointed out the difficulties in Nishida's theory. The infinite and its beyond, that is, absolute nothingness, must enter immediately into every operation where action takes place. However, in the account of absolute nothingness, given in *The Self-Aware System of the Universal*, Nishida assumes a basis of the self-aware system in a factorial manner by depicting absolute nothingness only as some-

---

12   *THZ*, 4: 327.

thing that exits at its deepest bottom. It is true that this account, by positing a difference in a hierarchical dimension, avoids the difficulty of infinity as a flat expansion of the present given in *An Inquiry Into the Good*. Nonetheless, if the infinite beyond is depicted as a bottomless bottom, it can only be understood as a limit that is somehow assumed in a spatial way, as something that envelops everything. Insofar as this is so, it cannot escape Tanabe's criticism that this is reducible to Plotinism, which explains everything as emanating in a hierarchical and structural manner from an ineffable one that has no relation to the scene of action. What then can Nishida do?

Nishida's answer is to embed absolute nothingness—the beyond, the transcendent—into action while maintaining its transcendence. Instead of positing absolute nothingness as a vertical bottom in the beyond, he reconsiders it to be something that slides in horizontally, as it were, into the scene where actions take place. Nothingness intervenes in the "here and now" in such a way as to destroy it from the inside.

After *The Self-Aware Determination of Nothingness*, Nishida develops his thought along the keywords of "death," the "Other," and the "discontinuity" within the "continuous." These are clearly new terms that had not been emphasized before in Nishida's philosophy of life. In addition to the introduction of these terms, his use of dialectical reasoning also becomes conspicuous. Death and the Other are forms of intervention employed by the transcendent aspect of nothingness within the scene of the "here and now," as in a rupture. Such an idea expresses a significant shift in Nishida's thoughts concerning absolute nothingness.

The Opposition Between the Species and the Individual

Leaving the details of this development of Nishida's thought for later, let us examine how Nishida's response to Tanabe brings into relief the difference between the thought of the two men. We will thereby be able to see in a vivid way Nishida's stance towards philosophy.

As is apparent from the fact that he developed a "logic of species," Tanabe regarded the concept of "species" to be fundamental in grasping reality. What is this logic of species? What kind of difference in Nishida's vision of philosophy does it express? Tanabe describes the species as a "mediator" between the individual and genus within the logical structural depicted according to the dialectical stages of individual species and genus; it is that which connects and establishes the particular and universal. For example, the concept of individual as a particular signifies the individual person; as a species, it signifies the "race" that mediates the particular and the universal; and as a universal genus, it expresses the "nation" that raises the race to the "position of humanity." Here, Tanabe emphasizes the importance of the reality of the species that mediates between the individual and genus. In other words, for Tanabe, the mediating species is the real *par excellence*. Therefore, to put it simply, Tanabe's theory is a theory of the "mediator." The central idea is that, without the mediation of a mediator, we cannot even discuss the force of becoming.

While this kind of conception of species is originally biological, Tanabe, as we saw in the above example, specifically develops this theory in the context of the social (the race).[13] If we consider the species as a mediator (and if we emancipate this concept from Tanabe's account and consider it in the context of Nishida that I will discuss below), then we can insert "race" into it, or "language" or "body." When an individual performs some action within the totality (absolute nothingness), race, language, and body all play the role of a mediator that explains this action. To use Tanabe's expression in "Request for Professor Nishida's Guidance," this kind of mediator is something contained within "relative history." The idea of the mediator is that we cannot say anything meaningful about force without passing through a "relatively" established mediator.

Nishida, however, does not assume the priority of this kind of mediating agent or species. For him, nothingness is given directly and *immediately* to the individual. Intensive force must be lived as a direct and immediate system. The mediator, the relative history, will certainly exist there. However, this must be spoken of from the encounter with the infinity of the flow, which is like a naked presentation of

---

13   Cf. "Shu no Ronri to Sekaizushiki" (The Logic of the Species and the World-Schema) in *Tanabe Hajime Zenshū* (Complete Works of Tanabe Hajime), Vol. 6 (Tokyo: Chikuma, 1936).

force. Therefore, Nishida does not speak from the side of the media-tor as Tanabe does. Instead, he attempts to describe becoming from the immediate, the "deep internal life" of the individual, the absolute nothingness. There, the individual is always directly connected with the totality (absolute nothingness).

Yet the mediate will become an important theme in the follow-ing development of Nishida's thought. The very fact that he begins to discuss the "discontinuity of the continuous" can in a sense be interpreted as indicating a shift of position regarding the continuity of the flow in his theory of intensive magnitude. When he discusses acting intuition, mediate things such as the body, language, and his-tory become major themes.[14] There, he begins mentioning the con-cept of species directly. Obviously, he has Tanabe strongly in mind.

Nonetheless, the difference between the two men never disap-peared. Even in his theory of acting intuition, what is important for Nishida is the becoming of the species. Thus, while accepting Tan-abe's critique, he continues to ask how the becoming of the mediate is possible. He recognizes the existence of the mediate, but he does not speak from its side. What is real is the force of becoming. Even if the force of becoming passes through the mediate, what Nishida's philosophy tries to describe is the force, the flow of life. Can the force of becoming only be spoken of from the side of the mediator, or will speaking of the force of becoming *ipso facto* be the same as speaking of the mediator? These two positions reflect two fundamentally differ-ent attitudes to philosophy. Tanabe always assumes the reality of the mediator. Nishida, keeping Tanabe in his mind, accepts the notion of the mediator and shifts his position, but continues trying to describe the force of becoming.

Absolute nothingness is the limit that is posited, where the domain of the virtual and intensive forces reach infinity. Even after his theory that posits this limit at the base of the flow was subject to criticism, Nishida continued to confront the force itself, seeking dif-ferent methods of description.

---

14   See especially *Tetsugaku Ronbunshū Daini* (Philosophical Papers Vol. 2).

The Significance of the Self-Aware Determination of Nothingness

Even after Tanabe's critique, Nishida does not abandon his concept of absolute nothingness in *The Self-Aware Determination of Nothingness*. This is clear from the following opening passage:

> At the base of what is conceived as reality must be something that is conceived as thoroughly irrational. Something that is merely rational cannot be real. However, even if the irrational is irrational, insofar as it is conceived, we must explicate how it is conceived.[15]

The issue is how to discuss the "irrational" absolute nothingness. As I have already mentioned, in the latter half of *The Self-Aware System of the Universal*, Nishida begins emphasizing the acting universal and expressive universal as that which the intelligible world is a part. What is conceived of as the intelligible is absorbed into the themes of expression and action. Nishida begins *The Self-Aware Determination of Nothingness* with this discussion and makes clear the direction of his thinking. He emphasizes that the theory of place, which previously had the danger of being interpreted as a suspension of the flow, is in its development none other than a theory of action.

At the same time, what is important is that Nishida shifts his conception of absolute nothingness so as to make it clear that it belongs to the themes of expression and action. This signifies a shift from discussing the place of nothingness to the self-aware determination of nothingness. The theme of action now comes to the fore. This is also apparent from the following passage in the essay, "What I Mean by the Self-Aware Determination of Absolute Nothingness," which is clearly a response to Tanabe's critique:

> What I mean by the self-aware determination of absolute nothingness is not what we normally think of as self-consciousness pushed to its limit; nor is it something like a mere mystical experience that has nothing to do with what we call action and knowledge. On the contrary, it is through the Self-Aware Determination of Nothingness that we conceive of action, and acting determination is conceived as so-called self-aware determination.[16]

---

15   *NKZ*, 5: 3.
16   *NKZ*, 5: 107–8.

Nothingness is no longer regarded as something that merely envelops the acting. It is no longer depicted as a limit that lies beyond the intelligible. Rather, the irrational nothingness is reconceived as something that is contained within our actions and makes those actions possible. It is a nothingness enveloped in the "here and now"; it is reinterpreted as something that makes action relevant to the themes of becoming and *poiesis*. The issue of *poiesis* thus comes to the fore of Nishida's theory. The concept of nothingness has undergone a drastic transformation.

As I have already mentioned, what we should notice in *The Self-Aware Determination of Nothingness* is that themes linked with the discontinuity within the continuous, such as death and the Other, make an appearance. We should also note that the eternal now is discussed differently than Nishida's previous theory of time. These are themes that were either absent in Nishida's earlier texts, or carried a different weight in his arguments. This is very significant, for the eternal, death, and the Other are, in a sense, concrete expressions of absolute nothingness—that is, they express the content of the transcendent that lies in the beyond. At the same time, once the transcendent is concretized in this way, it is no longer depicted as the limit of that which envelops. Next, let us examine the themes suggested by this concretized nothingness.

The Eternal Now

Nothingness is no longer considered something transcendent placed in the beyond. The beyond is re-depicted as something immanent in action. It is no longer merely nothing. It is no longer the limit of negation. Rather, the beyond is reconceived as something immanent in action and sets those actions in motion. This way of discussing the matter exposes from within the force of nothingness as something positive.

There are two aspects in which this nothingness has undergone a topological transformation. The first is the theory of time discussed in the essay, "The Self-Determination of the Eternal Now." There, eternity and death are interpreted as something immanent in the "now" and "life." The other aspect is the theory of the Other presented in the essay, "The I and Thou." There the Other, depicted as "Thou," appears as a kind of transcendent contained within the "I."

Let us first examine the theory of time. The theory of time had already occupied a significant place in Nishida's writings. What is it that distinguishes these earlier discussions from the one in "The Self-Determination of the Eternal Now"? The answer is related to how the keyword "eternal now" is understood. What is the eternal now? Nishida describes it as follows: "the infinite past and infinite future disappear at the single point of the present."[17] He also frequently uses the expression "an infinite circle whose circumference is nowhere and center is everywhere":[18]

> The absolute present that determines all times can be said to be a self-aware determination of absolute nothingness whose circumference is everywhere and center is nowhere. In this sense, what is conceived as absolute nothingness can be said to be an eternal now that can start anywhere and can always pull, afresh at every instant, the infinite past and infinite future into the single point of the present. Time can be thought to arise as the self-determination of the eternal now.[19]

Let us expand the flow of time forever, through and through. On the one hand, this will lead to an infinite past, and on the other, an infinite future. Nishida's previous theory of time posited something that envelops this infinite flow in the beyond. This was depicted as absolute nothingness. There, all future and past were described as existing simultaneously with the present (just as Bergson's theory of pure duration had presented all past as simultaneous). Because the theory encompassed the infinite, it presented the simultaneous existence of all time, released from the specific anchoring point called the present, as something paradoxical.

However, when we think about this again, where does this simultaneous time that contains the beyond exist? It is not something that exists anywhere. Yet it is only the present that answers to this "not existing anywhere." Can this not be depicted as the limit (the eternal) being folded into the "now"? This reconceived present is not,

---

17   *NKZ*, 5: 143–4.
18   *NKZ*, 5: 148. The original passage of Pascal that Nishida cites has "sphere" instead of "circle."
19   *NKZ*, 5: 148.

of course, an aspect of actualization (to use Bergson's terminology), a cross section of the infinite flow. Again, it is not a present that is merely simultaneous with the past and future, as it was described previously by Nishida. Rather, the beyond placed at the limit of the past and future is here topologically transformed and the present contained within this beyond comes to the fore. An eternal now that contains the beyond within itself like a rupture comes to the fore. What is important here is no longer the place of nothingness, but the self-determination of nothingness required for the "now" to arise.

Thus, the "now" is no longer a mere fixed point within the flow and which actualizes the flow. The present that contains the beyond must be understood as a kind of non-place that contains within itself the infinity of the flow. This present is ubiquitous, so to speak, over-lapping with the infinity of the flow. This is why Nishida frequently uses the peculiar phrase "circle whose circumference is nowhere and center is everywhere" in discussing the eternal now. Since the eternal now contains the infinite within itself, its center is everywhere. But this also implies the complete absence of a center (an anchoring point called the "present"). The eternal now is like a present floating in the void. It is circle with no circumference to determine its center, and hence, whose center is everywhere. The eternal now thus depicts a present that can start anywhere, afresh at every instant.

The Life Containing Death, the I Containing the Other

This eternal time, considered in itself, bears a resemblance to death. Nishida writes as follows:

> A circle whose center is everywhere and circumference is nowhere, in its noe-matic aspect [objective aspect], determines itself as a circle whose center is abso-lutely denied. The noematic aspect of the self-awareness of absolute nothingness can be thought of as something like an aspect of Absolute Death whose center is nowhere; and the noetic aspect [acting aspect] can be thought of as something like an aspect of Absolute Life whose center is everywhere.[20]

---

20   *NKZ*, 5: 157.

Our every instant is at once death and life ....[21]

While the eternal now, as a life that contains death, is the nega-tion of itself in every instant, it is also the productivity of the present by which new things constantly arise. This overlaps with Freud's discussion in *Beyond the Pleasure Principle*. There, having defined desire as "repetition," Freud distinguishes two aspects of desire, namely, Eros (the desire for life) and Thanatos (the desire for death); and, in contrast to Eros, which is a repetition of life, he depicts Thanatos, which is (so to speak) a repetition of "not yet being born" as the fundamental root of consciousness. In contrast to Eros, which is the repetition of the existence of an organism, Thanatos is the repetition of the inorganic matter that the organ-ism used to be (before it was life), and as such, it is a repetition that breaks down the organism's form. The repetition of Thanatos can be depicted as something that weaves the infinitely extended end of life into life once again. Rather than expressing death itself, it links life with the production of something new while dismantling life by describing the intervention of death into life.

Freud's discussion connects with Nishida's theory, in that, for both, the present is a "now" that contains eternity (death) within itself, and for this reason, produces something new at every instant. Like Freud's Thanatos, Nishida's eternal now is a "continuum of the discontinuous" that enters the "inside," reversing the "ultimate" of the continuity of the flow, and thereby giving rise to the present that introduces a rupture. Furthermore, the eternal now, the life containing death, overlaps with the theme of the Other (other person). For example, Nishida writes: "in the dialectic of Absolute Negation, which is Absolute Death *sive* Life ... the self must contain within itself the Absolute Other ... the self becomes the Other by passing through its own bottom."[22] The Other is the manifestation of the fact that the self, which exists in the phase of the eternal now that appears as a determination of absolute nothing-ness, possesses the infinite within itself. The self, by virtue of its very

21   *NKZ*, 5: 161.
22   *NKZ*, 5: 297.

existence, is exposed to the Other in the form of absolute nothingness. The life that contains death is also a self that contains the Other.

The Other established in this way is immediately re-depicted in a concrete manner as the "other person" or "Thou." Here, Nishida's theory not only describes the Other that is an appearance in the inside of the infinite beyond, but is also posited as a theory of the Other encompassing a self/other relationship that can be developed in the context of the social. The previous quotation continues:

> This is because at the basis of the existence of the Self is the Other, and at the basis of the existence of the Other is the Self. The I and Thou are absolutely Other [with respect to each other]. There is absolutely no universal that subsumes both the I and Thou. Yet, the I is the I by virtue of its recognizing the Thou, and the Thou is the Thou by virtue of its recognizing the I. At the basis of the I is the Thou, and at the basis of the Thou is the I ....[23]

Here, the "I" and "other person" are depicted as absolutely Other with respect to each other. In no sense is there a common place between the "I" and other person. They are not comprehensible by virtue of subsumption under a common universal.

How, then, can the other person be understood? The answer is as follows: "I" possess within my very being a fissure carved by the infinite. From the outset, the Absolute Other intervenes in me as a discontinuity. And the other person that is the Other, namely, Thou, possesses within itself an Absolute Other, a place of non-place, in the same way that the "I" does. Thus, it is through this containment of the Other that the "I" and "Thou" can recognize each other and respond to each other. The "I" enters into a relationship with the other person while maintaining the infinite otherness of the other person. This is also how the realm of the social is established:

> True self-awareness, whereby we are thought to see the Absolute Other within ourselves, must be social ... The I and Thou recognize the Absolute Other in each of their own bases, and because they mutually move towards the Absolute Other, the I and Thou can be said to be at once the Absolute Other and internally moving towards each other.[24]

---

23   *NKZ*, 5: 297.
24   *NKZ*, 5: 306.

Nishida calls this relation-less relationship "dialectical." This signifies a mere mutual recognition of the self and other. Rather, it is because the Self contains the Other within itself, and the other person enters into this Other, that there can be any response between the Self and other person. Here, the theory of the other person is depicted as one aspect of living life as a "continuum of discontinuities."

What is important in the context of the eternal now is that the eternal (the beyond) enters into the scene of action called the "now." The "now" is eternal. And death is depicted as something that is within life. Furthermore, the other person is not something different from the Self. It is an Other that enters into the Self and makes the Self possible. As the "continuum of discontinuities," all of these express a discontinuity that enters the continuous and makes the continuous possible.

It is in the development of these ideas that Nishida is able to discern a path of internally going beyond Bergson's philosophy of life. Having pushed the notion of the continuity of the flow to its limit, Nishida does not consider the transcendent that appears at the limit to be beyond the act of seeing, but rather introduces a topological shift, thereby weaving the transcendent into the "here and now":

> What is truly called life is not a continuous internal development like Bergson's creative evolution, but must be a continuum of discontinuities. Only through death is life possible. The vital impetus must be intermittent.[25]

> What Bergson calls the self is merely an intuitive self and not an acting self. Bergson's self has no death; nor is it a truly living and enacting self ....[26]

These are not mere rejections of Bergson's theory. Rather, Nishida should be understood as tracing the logic of Bergson's philosophy of life to its end, and presenting the prospects of a theory of action that lies beyond that logic. This is a theory that goes from a scene of intuition where one sees to a scene of action where one "enacts." As we shall see in the following section, this is a development that goes one step beyond a philosophy of life that adheres to life and its intensive forces.

---

25   *NKZ*, 5: 278–29.
26   *NKZ*, 5: 346.

The New Development of the Theory of Individuals

Considering the path of development of Nishida's theory, it should
be clear that the developments outlined above are extremely alien
compared to Nishida's earlier theory. These developments indicate a
transition that will lead us directly to Nishida's late philosophy. Especially important in considering this transition is the shift in the way
Nishida speaks of individuals.

As regards the theories of pure experience and self-awareness, the
individual could only be grasped from the side of the totality, the
infinite flow. The phase of the individual could only be approached
by asking how it could be detached from the totality within which
it initially exists. As to the theory of place, the individual was conceived only as something rooted in the predicate aspect, as something
that can be a predicate but never a subject. The focus of the theory of
the multi-layered place was to depict in a thorough way "that which
envelops" the basis of the flow. The radicalization of this idea results
in absolute nothingness.

However, during the period in which Nishida begins to conceive
of the absolute nothingness as a "continuum of discontinuities"
that intervenes in the scene of action, the concept of the individual
clearly undergoes a transition. Here, the individual is reconceived
as something standing in a reciprocal relation with the universal, as
something that makes discourse about the universal possible. The
individual is re-depicted as the subject of action involving nothingness, and thereby emerges as an independent phase: "the individual is
conceived to determine the universal, and the universal is conceived
to determine the individual";[27] "there is no individual without the
environment, and there is no environment without the individual."[28]

In the context of where the individual is presented in itself, we
can see a further radical transition in Nishida's manner of discussion.
From the theory of pure experience to the theory of place, what was
in the foreground of Nishida's discussion was the philosophy of life
itself, something that ought to be called the total affirmation of real-

---

27   *NKZ*, 5: 252.
28   *NKZ*, 5: 270.

ity. There, the intensive forces of the infinite flow were considered as something that ought to be affirmed through and through. And while the theory of place reaches the beyond of an ineffable absolute nothingness, insofar as the absolute nothingness itself is defined as something that "envelops," its reality was something that could only be apprehended through affirmation. However, when absolute nothingness is interwoven into the present and with the self as death and the Other, that is, when Nishida begins discussing the "continuum of discontinuities," it begins to bear a shadow of negation.

Thus frames Nishida criticism of Bergson's philosophy of life, which does not contain "death" or "discontinuities."[29] Specifically, Nishida argues that, in Bergson's theory, no evidence is given for "spatial determination," and that the individual or self is not depicted as a "working self." He further claims that a "dialectical" moment mediated by negation is necessary. The moment of negation is also depicted as something indispensable in the discussion of the determination of individuals involving nothingness.

Negation Drives the Individual from Within

While Nishida shifted his way of speaking, the negation that he introduces is not merely an "outer" negation. The intervening negation is rather a negation that enters into the being of the individual (the being of the "I") and drives it from within. Thus, the phase in which the individual—discussed within the mutual relation between the universal and environment—is affirmed is itself shifted. The object of affirmation becomes "that which moves" by itself through negation. Thus, what comes to the fore is the individual that moves by itself by virtue of its containing death within itself: "but we must not forget that it is by dying as individuals that we become moving individuals";[30] "in order for the individual to move as an individual from point to point, it must destroy itself."[31]

---

29   *NKZ*, 5: 278–29, 281–82, 346.
30   *NKZ*, 5: 229.
31   *NKZ*, 5: 231.

The individual is described from the perspective of dialectical opposition, as a "continuum of discontinuities" that contains death and the Other within itself. It is an "acting individual" that contains its own destruction within itself and creates new things—in short, a subject of *poiesis*. Thus, while this account of the individual makes clear the insufficiency of the point reached by the philosophy of life, it approaches in an even clearer manner the scene of "action" and the nature of life as *poiesis* that the "philosophy of life" was originally aiming at. As we shall see in more detail later, here we can see a parallel with the development of Deleuze's philosophy of life; namely, after criticizing Bergson for resting content at the stage of pure duration (which corresponds to the stage of the theory of place in Nishida), Deleuze posits the "temporality of Thanatos" (the "third synthesis of time") and goes toward the scene of becoming itself.

What we must discuss from here on is the world of *poiesis* constituted by individuals. The notion of "moving individuals" that contains death is already the first step into Nishida's late theory, which directly discusses *poiesis* as an action involving a "paradox."

5

ACTING INTUITION
The World of *Poiesis*

The World of Individuals

In *The Self-Aware Determination of Nothingness*, Nishida enacted a topological development wherein the absolute nothingness, which had been conceived as a bottomless "transcendent," is pinned down within action. Absolute nothingness is no longer conceived of as bottomless; rather, it reemerges as the "self-aware determination of nothingness," as a discontinuity that constitutes a continuum. From there, Nishida moves toward a world completely made of individuals—a world where individuals scatter and float on nothingness, where individuals constantly define each other while containing the totality within themselves.

In a vast collection of late essays bearing the uninspiring title, *Philosophical Essays*, Nishida discusses the nature of this world of individuals from various angles. Let us begin by examining his notion of the individual. We will take a look at some passages of texts included in Vols. 1 and 2 of *Philosophical Essays* that deal with acting intuition (e.g., "The Standpoint of Acting Intuition," "Acting Intuition"). For instance, he writes:

> The individual must be something that determines itself. An individual cannot be thought as something wholly singular; it is an individual only in relation to another individual. Here, we must suppose that there is a mediating continuum of discontinuities ... For an individual to determine itself is for the part to contain the whole, and for a thing to become its own mediator.[1]

---

1   *NKZ*, 7: 88–89.

> It is the mediating continuum of discontinuities that is conceived as the "total-
> ity." When things are independent of each other and yet bond with each other,
> each of these are conceived to contain the significance of the totality.[2] (7–104)

> The world in which individuals determine each other is a world where [individu-
> als] develop themselves in original ways, from the created to the creating.[3]

What is at issue here is no longer the "I" that is situated by being
subsumed under the totality of the flow. Nor is it a totality with a
phase difference, a place that envelops such individuals. Rather, the
individual itself acts by interacting with other individuals; and the
totality that reaches nothingness through this action is itself subsumed as a mediating "continuum of discontinuities." The immediate
flow that Nishida had been illustrating is thereby weaved into the side
of the acting individual as a kind of mediator.

That is, the individual is no longer depicted from the side of the
totality of the flow. Rather, the totality of the flow enters into the
individual by carving fissures, and through these fissures the individual acts toward other individuals and vice versa, in each instance creating something new. The individual which is a part contains within
itself the whole, so to speak, maintaining the latter's beyondness. And
through the paradox that is thereby exposed, the individual executes
actions involving other individuals. Such individuals are not only
"created," but are also creating themselves.

This kind of individual can be said to be the "acting" self; it is "that
which acts." And through each of its acts, the acting self "expresses"
the world (the totality), and at the same time, through its very being,
it creates the world (the totality) as something new. This act of creating something new is what Nishida calls acting intuition. The world
of *poiesis* is thus illustrated:

> I see a thing by acting; the thing determines me and I determine the thing. This
> is acting intuition.[4]

---

2   *NKZ*, 7: 104.
3   *NKZ*, 8: 208.
4   *NKZ*, 7: 11.

> Intuition is the self-determination of the expressive world. It is the seeing of a thing through action. This is how the thing is created. This is the world of *poiesis* ... The taking place of intuition, to see something through action, is the mutual expressive determination of countless things.[5]

What Nishida calls acting intuition is not a merely passive state as the word intuition may suggest; it is not merely an act of seeing. As I have already mentioned, to "see" in this context is to see the infinite. It is to see the totality as something containing ruptures within itself. Thus, the act of seeing is *ipso facto* an expression of the infinite itself, and is linked with the acting or *poiesis*. The action of creative individuals where "to act is to see, and to see is to act"[6]—this is acting intuition. In acting intuition, the individual determines what it is through its mutual relation with other individuals and at the same time; it defines what the world and other individuals are.

Life Depicted by Individuals

How should we imagine such individuals? In order to answer this question, we must consider the fact that in his discussion of acting intuition, Nishida approaches the themes of history and art closer than he ever had done before. In particular, he emphasizes historically significant actions and instances of artistic creation. This is because these are cases where the actions of each individual lead to the creation of history and objects of art. However, I believe that what Nishida calls the individual at this stage should be understood as life. Why? Because life is something that moves by itself, just as in Nishida's model of acting intuition. Life is something that moves by itself, determines itself, and at the same time creates the world.

Let us think about this. An organism determines its own nature by moving by itself. Self-movement is related to genes (the internal environment). The cell that is the self is also related to the various pieces of matter in which it is nurtured (the external environment). It is further related to various individuals existing in its surroundings

---

5   *NKZ*, 7: 121.
6   *NKZ*, 7: 122.

(the Other). An organism can be a self only by virtue of its existing within such a nexus. Without such a nexus, an organism as an individual, cannot take shape. In this sense, the organism is something that is created by various relations. An organism can move by itself first and foremost as something created.

The genes, environment, and other individuals exist "here and now." They cannot exist independently of the initial individual. On the contrary, insofar as they are each conceived of as individuals, they are dependent upon the individual organism existing "here and now," regardless of the manner of dependence. Their existence is reciprocal. Take genes as an example. For an individual organism, its genes are certainly something given. But the genes can exist only by virtue of there being an individual organism that moves by itself—only by virtue of the individual's expressing those genes. Furthermore, the individual is an organism that moves by itself and creates its genes by entering into relations with other individuals (in one sense, through reproduction). Each individual, in its being an individual, expresses the presence of its genes. It is something that bestows a difference upon its genes and diversifies their existence. In this sense, the individual creates its genes through its own very existence. Yet at the same time, the individual recombines its genes by interacting with other individuals. It specifically creates new genes. Thus, in these two senses, the individual in its very being as something that moves, shifts from the created to that which creates.

While the internal and external environment of the organism, as well as other individuals, are things (individuals) that create individuals, they are in one respect created by individuals. They cannot exist unless individuals exist. Insofar as the individual is something that moves by itself, it is a scene where new things are created. This shift from the "created" to that which "creates" is the first point that should be highlighted in Nishida's theory of acting intuition.

Now, having organized the structure of acting intuition in this way, how should we depict it? I believe that there are three points that ought to be emphasized. The first is that, while the individual is something that is "created," it is also something that "creates," and in this sense, the individual cannot be spoken of except as a boundary indicating the identity of contradictories. Hence, acting intuition always involves the notion of "dialectic." It must always be a theory of an intertwining of a boundary and its opposite.

The second point that ought to be emphasized is that the individual is what produces reality. The individual is something that expresses the totality, but this act of expressing is not something ideal. Rather, it is the *poiesis* of reality, the production of new life and the recombination of genes.

Third, in the context of acting intuition as something that produces reality, new themes that Nishida had not previously discussed come to the fore. These are the themes of body, history, and species, which had not been very conspicuous in Nishida's earlier writings. These themes, which are, in a sense, concrete mediators for the individual enter into the discussion of becoming.

Mutually Mediating Worlds

Let me begin by discussing the individual as a boundary that indicates the identity of contradictories. From the outset, Nishida's account of the individual itself involves an aspect of contradiction. This can be seen more than anything else in the very term "acting intuition." To act is to work, and to intuit is to see. Usually, to act is something active, while to intuit is gives the impression of something passive. From the outset, these two terms do not go well together.

The term "acting intuition" transgresses the boundary between the active and the passive and brings them together effortlessly. What is important in this concept is that to act is itself to intuit and to work is itself to see. To repeat what I said before, "a thing is seen through action," and "to see is to act."[7] This immediately leads to a shift from the "created" to that which "creates." What we see here is the transformation of the passive into the active.

In the theory of the intelligible world, the act of seeing the infinite was conceived as the limit of an intensive state that is revealed in intuition. Here, this seeing is described as an act involving concrete things, an interplay in which one participates in an extensive state from within. In other words, the phase of intuition related to intensive magnitude, which had previously been described as a vertical depth, is no longer extracted by itself. Rather, the theory of acting intuition describes an interplay in which the phase of intuition enters into the horizontal horizon related to extensive magnitude, and, as a concrete act, displays the function of the identity of contradictories. The intuition in which one sees nothingness is transformed into action, all the while retaining its nature.

In the context of acting intuition, Nishida gives the boundary-like account that overlays two domains in this manner in various ways:

> The self must be an acting self. True temporality is conceived where internal perception is external perception and external perception is internal perception.[8]

> The self-identity of time and space lies where the internal is the external, the external is the internal, the subjective is the objective, and the objective is the subjective. Real time and space arise henceforth as two opposing sides of dialectical self-identity.[9]

> Evidently, time is space and space is time; individual determination is universal determination and universal determination is individual determination. Therefore, internal unity and external unity must be identical through and through.[10]

> Dialectic lies where the immanent is transcendent and the transcendent is immanent, where absolute opposites are self-identical.[11]

Nishida employs these instances of the identity of contradictories, the enumeration of which would be an endless task, to express the nature of acting intuition. What Nishida wants to claim in these expressions is the interplay between the two words of the phrase acting intuition.

What Nishida is discussing in his theory of acting intuition is the intrusion from within of what is depicted as a vertical depth (the internal, the subjective, the temporal, the universal, the predicate, the intensive) into what is described as a horizontal horizon (the external,

---

8   *NKZ*, 7: 86.
9   *NKZ*, 7: 87.
10   *NKZ*, 7: 90.
11   *NKZ*, 7: 95.

the objective, the spatial, the individual, the [grammatical] subject, the extensive) by a "continuum of discontinuities." The discussion that seeks the infinity of the intensive flow enters into extensive spatial determination itself in an intermingling manner, thereby depicting the identity of contradictories.

As I mentioned before, this is an indication of a major shift in Nishida's thought. From the theory of pure experience to the theory of absolute nothingness, he was completely preoccupied with rejecting the extensive that can be depicted spatially and with illustrating the intensive—the continuity of the flow—in which the extensive is originally rooted. However, when he comes to take up the issue of acting intuition, he begins to discuss the constant interplay between the forces that constitute life vertically and the state where these forces are spatialized horizontally and represented. The flow enters into the individual as the identity of contradictories. The individual is thus a boundary where such contradictions arise.

Therefore, becoming is no longer described as the actualization of the virtual, the "formless" becoming "form." Rather, what is important here is the transition from the "actual" to the "actual." To anticipate what I will discuss in the following chapter on the absolute contradictory self-identity,[12] it is the unfolding of a "form" to a "form":

> The virtual does not exist outside of the manifest, but is contained within the self-contradictions of the actual.[13]

> The actual does not consist in a mere transition from the virtual to the manifest; it is a transition from reality to reality. It is a transition from intuition to intuition; it is to constantly touch the Absolute.[14]

> The world of the Absolute contradictory self-identity that infinitely moves from the created to that which creates is through and through a formative action from form to form.[15]

---

12 In terms of content, the self-identity of absolute contradictories is the same as the theory of acting intuition. The basic principles of the self-identity of absolute contradictories have already been laid down.

13 *NKZ*, 8: 81.

14 *NKZ*, 8: 84–85.

15 *NKZ*, 8: 375.

But this may be obvious. For the world depicted by the theory of acting intuition is a world of extensive individuals that receive the flow of life, a place that constantly creates new forms. What Nishida is then describing by his term "world of the dialectical universal" is a situation where contradictory things intermingle and go beyond each other. The word "dialectic" is, of course, taken from Hegel. But for Nishida, the word does not have the Hegelian sense of the sublation of contradictories. For Nishida, a contradiction is not an occasion for going a step beyond. Rather, contradictory things remain identical; here, Nishida is depicting the arising of this intermingling. For Nishida, the word "dialectic" is used to describe the real world that develops endlessly from "reality" to "reality" from "form" to "form," without ever reaching ultimate settlement.

The Individual as Poiesis

What we must take up next in the context of individuals is the fact that individuals produce reality. Individuals make (*poieo*) reality. In other words, to be at the boundary between intensive and extensive magnitude as the identity of contradictories is to move from "reality" to "reality," to create or make (*poieo*) reality.

Acting intuition is in one respect an expression. It is the expression by the individual of the infinite itself. But the individual creates the world as something real in the way it expresses (determines) the infinite: "living consists not in emotions or mystical intuition, but in objective creation";[16] "in addition, true action is *poiesis*, and our actions transform the outer world. They create things."[17] The "acting" in acting intuition should always be understood from the standpoint of creation, which denotes *poiesis*, or objective creation itself. To create is to make a form. There are two implications of this.

The first is that creation is always a reciprocal act: it is the mutual determination of two individuals or the mutual action of the individual and world. Here, we can see that the individual cannot be

---

16   *NKZ*, 8: 4.
17   *NKZ*, 8: 11.

depicted as anything other than that which acts at the boundary with other individuals or the world. It is thus emphasized that that which "creates" is also "created." For example, the last quote continues: "the created thing is independent, and as a thing, it determines us."[18] Here, Nishida is claiming that the created object is itself an individual, and as such determines the self that created it. He describes the world of individuals as the interplay of the subjective and objective as follows: "in action, the self moves the thing and the thing moves the self; the subject determines the object and the object determines the subject."[19]

The individual lies at the boundary between the self and other individuals (things). It is at the boundary between the self and the world (the objective). The individual creates things through mutual determination with other individuals. The individual creates things in the world. Acting intuition is in one respect to create oneself and other individuals (that which "creates"). But that is not all. The self is at the same time created by the individuals that it creates (the "created"). Creation is always a reversible and reciprocal act between that which creates and the created.

Again, the individual creates things by moving the world (the objective). To create is to create oneself in the world and to create something in the world. But in this act of creation, the self is at the same time created by being moved by the world. In the *poiesis* of individuals, the subjective and objective are described as such a mutual interplay. The self's creation of itself overlaps with the world's creation of the world.

The Creation of Reality

The second implication is that, in the creation of reality and the making of a form, the creation of something new is always involved. What is created cannot be a mere material repetition. In one respect, to create something is to repeat it, looking back to the past. However, in

18   *NKZ*, 8: 11.
19   *NKZ*, 7: 99.

acting intuition the "continuum of discontinuities," a rupture is always involved in this very repetition. This is what Nishida means by the eternal now. His discussion of objective creation shows that this aspect of creation always involves this kind of rupture:

> To be truly creative, one must contain Absolute Negation within oneself; the spatial must deny the temporal and the temporal must deny the spatial. The truly creative must display the function of formation.[20]

The novelty that is created is not a peculiar kind of experience. It is true that the typical kinds of situation described by the theory of acting intuition involve actions in the context of history, art, and life. It is in this kind of situation that a new reality is created in a visible manner. But at the same time, what we must consider is that acting intuition constitutes the content by which we feel that reality is real: a movement of the fingertip, or a movement of the arm, for example. Any subtle movement will do. To say that such a movement is real is to say that it reflects the world itself in a manner however subtle— that it is a creation wherein the infinite flow intervenes as a rupture. This is what it means to say that the self and world are in the process of reciprocally creating a new reality.

Now in this context, Nishida begins to say many things about the themes of the body (tools and language) and history.[21] He also begins to discuss the theme of the species from a new angle.[22] The emergence of these themes can be seen as an indication that Nishida, who up until now had been discussing immediate becoming, has changed his mode of discussion. In other words, these themes are concrete manifestations of a kind of mediator that arises when one conceives of the scene of becoming as acting intuition in the interplay between intensive magnitude and extensive magnitude, and attempts to deal

---

20   *NKZ*, 8: 38.
21   "Logic and Life" in *Tetsugaku Ronbunshū Daini* (Philosophical Papers Vol. 2), is particularly important as a theory of the body and history. [An English translation of this essay is included in *Place and Dialectic: Two Essays by Nishida Kitarō*, trans., John W. M. Krummel and Shigenori Nagatomo (Oxford: Oxford University Press, 2011).]
22   The concept of species is discussed in "Logic and Life" and "The Issue of the Genetic Development of Species," also included in *Tetsugaku Ronbunshū Daini*.

with the production of reality therein. We must keep in mind that for Nishida, the themes of body, history, and species are to be approached from this kind of perspective.

Body and History

Acting intuition is a scene where the self makes a thing and a thing makes the self. Such a scene where the self makes a thing and a thing makes the self is a bodily one. Without a body, the acting subject cannot interact with the thing. Creation requires a body:

> Without a body, there can be no self. Yet we have a body as a tool. Our body is also something that is seen from the outside. Yet our body is not only something that is seen; it is also that which sees. Without a body there can be no seeing.[23]

In this passage, Nishida describes the body as something that is at once "seen" (making it a thing) and "sees" (making it a subject), and, in this sense, as the marginal interplay itself between individuals. It is a tool by which the individual enacts acting intuition.

Nishida also describes the body as follows: "our body is an organ that rationalizes the irrational. We have our body as a tool, and at the same time we are bodily beings through and through."[24] The "irrational" that leads to absolute nothingness is presented by the vertical depth of the intensive flow. Nishida depicts the body as a marginal tool that unfolds this "irrational" into a horizontal horizon and rationalizes it in a spatial manner.

It is through our bodies that our actions create reality. We concretely create things and we in turn function as things created by these things. And the scene into which our bodies intervene and create things is, according to Nishida, historical. The body is first and foremost biological. Yet the body is not only a tool (functioning as acting intuition); it is also something that makes tools (Nishida says that this is what characterizes humans; see *NKZ*, 8: 10). Further-

---

23   *NKZ*, 8: 49.
24   *NKZ*, 8: 47.

more, strongly linked to such tools is language.[25] Hence, the body is a biological organ that creates things in coordination with others, within a network of technology. It is in this sense that Nishida says that the creation of reality is a historical act. The body is a historical body. Thus, he discusses practice in the "historical world" on the basis of the body, which is what plays the role of acting intuition:

> Our self is historical because it is bodily. I believe it is through the analysis of that which is most immediately given to us, namely our bodies, that we will be able to grasp the dialectical nature of historical reality.[26]

> Our bodies are historical bodies. We possess not only hands but also language. To act historically and bodily is to immerse oneself into the historical world; and only insofar as this is a self-determination of the expressive world can we be said to be acting and enacting. Our bodily self is a creative element within the historical world; historical life realizes itself through our bodies.[27]

The themes of body, tools, and language—themes that Nishida had not discussed before—here come to the fore in a lavish way. But this is only because he is developing the interplay between intensive magnitude and extensive magnitude, between irrational forces and the rational horizon. In this sense, the themes of body and history take on the role of a kind of mediator against the immediacy of life. When thinking of the boundary at which individuals are situated, these themes must be considered as mediators peculiar to such boundaries.

Life as Species

Here, the discussion links with the theme of species. On the one hand, Nishida conceives of species as biological species. But on the other hand, he also discusses species in the historical sense, namely, in the sense of ethnic groups. When one conceives of the body—at once biological and historical—as the scene of acting intuition, one thereby makes the concept of species, which can be discerned within

---

25   *NKZ*, 8: 24–25.
26   *NKZ*, 8: 4.
27   *NKZ*, 8: 47.

the body itself as an object of examination. To create biologically and historically is *ipso facto* an act of the species—it is to pass through the mediator of the species:

> To immerse oneself in the world ... is rather to push oneself to the bottom of the body. It is therefore not to reject or ignore the species, but to pass through the species. It is to make the species a mediator. To pass through the species means to be born and work as a species.[28]

Nishida's introduction of the theme of species—and in particular the way he brings in the topic of the "mediator"—reminds one of Tanabe's critique mentioned previously. Nishida's discussion of the concept of species is clearly informed by Tanabe's "logic of species," including the way in which he relates the concept to social phenomena. In one respect, Nishida seems to be embracing the theme that Tanabe had been discussing.

However, Nishida's account is quite different from Tanabe's notion of the mediator. For Nishida, the species is certainly a mediator, but it is not something real. The species is constituted by the individuals that live at the boundaries, but Nishida's question is how the species intervenes into the scene of becoming. To be sure, Tanabe had also been dealing with the logic of species in this sense. But what Nishida's interest lies in the "genetic development" of the species involved in the life of the individuals. These species have significance only insofar as they function as mediators for action, but only insofar as they genetically develop with the acting. Nishida's theory is consistent in this respect:

> Various species can be said to arise as the self-determination of the dialectical universal. Therefore, the species lives by world-historically negating itself. The procession of history must be an individual procession rather than a continuity of species.[29]

> The individual must be something that is internally mediated. It lives precisely for that reason. The individual must be species-like. The subject determines the environment, and the environment determines the subject. In order to say that

---

28   *NKZ*, 8: 47.
29   *NKZ*, 8: 190.

the species lives as a dialectical self-identity, one must say that it makes the individual a mediator.[30]

Acting intuition is a world where individuals create reality by entering into relations with other individuals. Insofar as this is so, the individual possesses a rupture within itself whereby various things are mediated in that rupture. This is where the body comes into the account. We said previously that the body is something that acts and that Nishida considers it to be historical. Moreover, in history, there is the concept of species. Accordingly, he depicts the species as the necessary for the existence of the individual; it is an element that constitutes reality.

However, Nishida does not think that the species has an independent existence. The species is a "living species,"[31] but its existence can be spoken of only with reference to the scene of acting intuition performed by individuals. It is only on the basis of the reality that is newly and constantly created by individuals that the meaning of the mediator can be spoken of. The species is, therefore, something that is in the making in the scene of becoming in conformity with the *poiesis* of individuals. The body is such a thing, and so is history. The mediator must be depicted as something that touches the force of becoming possessed by the work of individuals.

In other words, while the concept of the mediator comes to the fore in Nishida's account, it is described as something that is exposed to the irrational force of life itself. Although it is the mediator of the *poiesis* of individuals, it is a mediator that is in the making only insofar as it is always in conformity with the *poiesis* of individuals.

---

30   *NKZ*, 8: 206.
31   *NKZ*, 8: 206.

6

ABSOLUTE CONTRADICTORY SELF-IDENTITY
The Logic of Becoming

The Contradictory Self-Identity of the Many and the One

If the world depicted by acting intuition is one that captures the repeated mutual inversion of the acting self, then what is described by the term "absolute contradictory self-identity" must be the "world in the making" itself created by the actions of the acting self.

The basic elements of the concept of absolute contradictory self-identity developed in *Philosophical Papers Vol. 3* (especially the essay "The Absolute Contradictory Self-Identity") and later works can already be seen in the notion of acting intuition. The issue at stake here is how to logicize the marginal nature of reality dealt with in acting intuition as an absolute self-identity of contradictories, and thereby organize and depict in simple way the actual world where individuals mutually determine individuals.

In the essay "The Absolute Contradictory Self-Identity," Nishida summarizes the identity of contradictories in terms of the "many" and the "one":

> This world must be a world that moves from the created to that which creates. It is not a world constituted by the mutual action of immutable atoms as in conventional physics; in other words, it is not a world that can be thought of as a unity of the many. Such a world would be nothing but a repetition of the same world. Nor can the world be conceived as a purposeful world, the development of a total unity. In such a world, there would be no mutual enacting of individuals. The world must be such that it can be conceived neither as the unity of the many, nor the multiplicity of the one.[1]

---

1 *NKZ*, 8: 367–68.

Nishida regards the depiction of the world as the "unity of the many" as "mechanical." It is a worldview that assumes an "individual multiplicity" (some kind of elemental things) that can exist on their own without mutual determination and constructs from these the "one" (the totality). On the other hand, Nishida regards the depiction of the world as the multiplicity of the one as teleological. It is a view that assumes a "total unity" prior to the existence of individual phenomena and sees the function of the world as a movement towards this "one."

The former view sees the world from the past to the future. It assumes some kind of concept of cause and effect and mechanically describes the world as an effect of the past. The latter view can be said to see the world from the future to the past. It posits from the outset a purpose that is assumed to be realized in the future by describing the world as a movement directed towards that purpose.

Nishida, however, does not regard the world of acting intuition, the world where individuals mutually determine each other, as a "unity of the many" or a "multiplicity of the one." There is no such thing as a "one" (an intensive totality) that exists at the base of the world. Nor is there a "many" (extensive individuals) that exists without relation to the world as a whole. The world as conceived by Nishida is one that develops from the "present" to the "present." It is a world where the "one" and the "many," the intensive and the extensive, are immediately linked together as the transition of the present:

> The world of the contradictory self-identity of the many and the one, the world where the created becomes that which creates, must be a world conceivable as a transition from the present to the present. The present has a form, and whatever is within the present must be determined through and through; that is, it must be real, and yet as something contradictory self-identically determined, it must be something that moves from its own self-contradiction.[2]

Just as in acting intuition, the world Nishida describes is world of moving individuals that carry out *poiesis* by mediating the totality (nothingness) within itself as a "continuum of discontinuities":

---

2   *NKZ*, 8: 370.

> When an individual, as an individual within a world of the contradictory self-identity of the many and one, reflects the world, the self-determination of the individual is a desire. The individual does not act mechanically or purposefully. It acts by reflecting the world within itself.[3]

The individual is not wholly prescribed by anything (whether it be a cause from the past or a purpose from the future) other than the fact that there is a present. It is true that in one respect individuals in the present are constrained by causation and purposefulness. It is because they are prescribed in this way that they arise as things having some kind of form.

The individual, however, is something into which the infinite past penetrates and contains within itself a rupture that looks forward into the infinite future; in this sense, although the individual is always in the present, it merely brims over into the present. What is real is this present. The present is that which reflects the world and constantly creates itself. What Nishida means by "desire" is the constantly shifting world of the present, which he also describes as "wavering." It is within the present that it is possible to talk about the past and future.

The World as a Task

A useful idea for thinking about the world as the absolute contradictory self-identity of the "many" and the "one" is Nishida's claim that the world is given as a "task." The reason that the world has a form is because a task has been solved in one way. But insofar as the world is task, there is no way that it can be ultimately solved. Even if one task is solved, an endless number of other tasks await. To live is to continue solving such tasks and to present an endless variety of solutions:

> Within the world of the absolute contradictory self-identity, whatever is given to us must be given to us as a task. We are obligated to create something in this world. Therein lies our life.[4]

---

3   *NKZ*, 8: 373.
4   *NKZ*, 8: 393.

To be born with a body—that itself means that we could say that one task has already been solved by historical nature (such as when we say that an insect's eyes have been created), but at the same time, as the absolute contradictory self-identity, it means that there is an infinite number of tasks contained therein. To say that we are born with a body is to say that we are born bearing an infinite number of tasks. Whatever is truly immediately given to our acting selves must be something that confronts us objectively as a solemn task.[5]

The world as a task and the example of its solution links directly with life. Here, Nishida takes up the discussion of biological evolution whereby the forms of bodies (such as the eyes of an insect) are constituted as a concrete example of *poiesis* in the present in response to a task.

Such accounts give a strong impression that Nishida's thought corresponds to the themes taken up by Bergson and Deleuze, for what Bergson and Deleuze contemplate is the world as given to us as a "problem." And the concrete example that they give of a solution to this problem is that of forms (especially eyes) acquired by evolution.[6] For an organism to have a form is to live this world with the infinite virtuality that it bears within itself. Bergson, in his original example (which Nishida probably had in mind), discusses the marvelousness of the fact that both mollusks and vertebrates, which belong to different evolutionary lineages, develop similar eye structures using different body parts. Bergson then goes on to argue that this opening up of vision cannot be explained either mechanistically or teleologically. Deleuze describes the creation of eyes as a solution to the problem of light. In other words, this is a world where light is given to us as a problem. To develop eyes is a way of responding to this problem. Organisms exist bearing an infinite virtuality within themselves. Thus, organisms that attempt to respond to the same problem of light can create similar sophisticated organs in different circumstances following different developmental paths. The eyes that are created in this way are one solution to the problem. For life to evolve and acquire forms is to solve problems in this fashion.

What we must also keep in mind is that even after eyes have been created, evolution does not stop there. Eyes are developed one after

---

5   *NKZ*, 8: 393.
6   Bergson takes up the example of eyes in *Creative Evolution*, while Deleuze discusses eyes as an example of solving a "problem" in *Difference and Repetition*.

another in each individual such that every instance of this is a historic solution of the problem that is the world on behalf of the species. However, the task of light is posed constantly. It is given as an infinite task. Therefore, in one circumstance, life may create a completely new kind of eye; it may develop a completely new organ of vision. But this is the task of the present where individuals "waver," for it is the present that creates each individual eye.

As long as it is living and moves by itself, life will not stop solving such problems. To continue solving the problem of light is what it means to live with the sense of vision. What we should emphasize is that both Nishida and Deleuze claim that this world of tasks or problems is objective existence. What is concretely given to us is the fact that the world is an infinite task or problem that can never be fully solved. The world is not something that has an ultimate answer somewhere. What is real is what is posed to us in the mode of being of a task or problem.

The scene of the absolute contradictory self-identity that moves from "actuality" to "actuality" is a scene where forms are created through the continued proposal of solutions to the task or problem of the world. But there is no ultimate answer. To be "actual" means that an individual with infinite virtuality, constantly confronting the infinite world, is infinitely wavering from "form" to "form." The world of the absolute contradictory self-identity is a scene where such individuals are given a rupture by infinity from within and waver from "present" to "present."

A Group-Theoretic World

In the last period of his life, when he begins to discuss absolute contradictory self-identity, Nishida once again begins referring to mathematics and discussions about its foundations. Although separated by time, his discussions during this last period overlap with those of the period of *Intuition and Reflection in Self-Awareness*, in which Nishida frequently referred to the differential and set theory.

From around the time of writing "Logic and Life," Nishida begins characterizing the nature of the absolute contradictory self-identity in terms of the algebraic concept of "groups." In *Philosophical Papers Vol. 6*, he devotes many pages to the examination of mathematical ideas, including physics and mathematical space. It seems that in his last period, after having discussed *poiesis*, which is directly related to life, Nishida attempts to apply his notion of the absolute contradictory self-identity to the more fundamental realm of mathematics. In an audacious maneuver, he even tries to ground mathematical discussions in the structure of the absolute contradictory self-identity, by which he claims that the part contains the whole and the self reflects itself.[7] How should we understand these references to mathematics? Here, we cannot go into a detailed discussion of group theory and set theory (that would require us to cover the basics of group theory and Cantor's discussions, and also examine the validity of Nishida's attempts to ground these; this, however, is a task beyond my capacities). Rather, let us organize the issues to the extent that it is necessary for our purposes.

Nishida's inclination towards the foundations of mathematics during this period is, in one respect, a result of the same perspective that had led him, in his discussion of self-awareness, to deal with the mathematics of infinity in order to logicize the extraction of the finite from the infinite realm of pure experience. To discuss the absolute contradictory self-identity is itself to contemplate the connection between the infinite and the finite. And it was the foundational theories of mathematics, represented by set theory, that provided rich ideas about infinity.

However, there is a difference in the manner of discussion between the absolute contradictory self-identity period and the self-awareness period. In the self-awareness period, the issue at stake was to understand how the self enters into infinity. The topic of the absolute contradictory self-identity period, on the other hand, is the intermingling of the infinite and the finite. This can be reinterpreted as the intermingling of the intensive and extensive. What is important here is to depict the scene of *poiesis*, where the infinite enters into the finite (individual). The theme

---

7   See for example "Logic and Life" and "The Philosophical Grounding of Mathematics" in *Tetsugaku Ronbunshū Dairoku* (Philosophical Papers Vol. 6).

here is how to deal with the infinity that the finite individual contains within itself like a rupture.

What Nishida calls "group-theoretic" and what he describes as "inverse determination" is related to this theme:

> The world must be such that, whenever this thing and that thing within the world link together (that is, work together) and create a new thing as a result, the new thing is also something within the world and works as a thing within the world; that is, the world must be a group-theoretic system. No matter how we work, we cannot go outside of the world. And whatever we create, the created thing is also a thing that works within this world. Thus, whatever rejects us must also be contained within the world (just like the inverse element of a group).[8]

> When the world where the totality expresses itself within itself as a contradictory self-identity of the many and one—what I have called the contradictory self-identical world—possesses an element within itself that expresses itself, that element can be thought of as a creative element, something that creates. It is just like the identity element of a mathematical group.[9]

What Nishida tried to claim using the term "group-theoretic" is that, in this world that moves from "form" to "form," from "present" to "present," every individual exists within the world (as an element of a group), and that everything that individuals create through their work also exists within the world (as an element of the group). Furthermore, Nishida's account is a formulation of the circumstance that such work is possible only when each (finite) individual relates infinitely with other individuals and bears the negation that arises from this infinite relation. Conversely, it is a presentation of the circumstance that, within the work of individuals, the world (the totality, the group system) reflects the self (the individual the group element) within itself as a "contradictory self-identity" of the "one" and the "many" and comes into being as something creative.

This is related to the expression "inverse-determination" that Nishida uses in connection to group theory:

---

8   *NKZ*, 8: 38.
9   *NKZ*, 10: 242.

The one-to-one correspondence between individuals also compels itself to be understood in a way different from the usual sense. Usually, people regard two forms in a parallel manner, and consider a one-to-one correspondence between the elements of the two forms. They consider a mutual correspondence between individuals on an objective plane, so to speak. However, in the case of a form that determines itself in a contradictory self-identical way, two individuals must fundamentally and through and through have the significance of an inverse-determination with respect to each other; they must have the significance of mutual negation.[10] (10–193,194)

While the correspondence between individuals can exist only as a correspondence between two forms (and, in this sense, each individual must be a determined element), the individuals in such a correspondence have passed through a mutually negating mediation via the infinity of relationships. Thus, they can only be depicted in terms of an "inverse correspondence" that negatively contains each within the other. While the individuals are absolutely other with respect to each other, they can only ever be presented in the intermingled manner of reflecting the sameness of infinity (of being a self-determination of the same infinity). Nishida further considerations of set theory from this "infinite inverse-correspondence between individuals" requires attention.[11]

Finite Numbers and Infinite Numbers

Nishida's way of speaking about the relation between cardinal numbers and ordinal numbers mentioned in the chapter on self-awareness also undergoes a transition in his late period. In the self-awareness period, Nishida had only claimed the priority of ordinal numbers, which are strongly related to intensive infinity. In his late period, however, he begins discussing the intermingling of the ordinal and the cardinal on the basis of the contradictory identity of natural numbers.

The discussion is developed as follows. Nishida introduces finite numbers, which are an extensive way of counting numbers, and infi-

---

10   *NKZ*, 10: 193–94
11   *NKZ*, 10: 194.

nite numbers, which are numbers related to intensive infinity. Finite numbers are natural numbers, which are countably infinite (denumerable to infinity); basically, they are cardinal numbers. Infinite numbers, generally speaking, are real numbers, which are uncountably infinite (that is, indenumerable—they are numbers that express a dense infinity of real numbers, including irrational numbers); they are ordinal numbers. Nishida does not even say that the former are cardinal numbers nor that the latter are ordinal numbers. All he says is that, by both being natural numbers, they intermingle as a contradictory identity:

> But the natural numbers are already infinite. They are already a contradictory self-identity of the inside and outside. ... Furthermore, finite numbers are thought within infinite numbers. Finite numbers are also ordinal. ... Yet, within the closed circle of self-awareness, ordinal numbers and cardinal numbers are one.[12]

> Beyond the natural numbers, we can think of ordinally endless infinite numbers ... However, they are through and through within the circle of self-awareness, and can never depart from acting-intuitional determination. ... That is, they must be fused with the natural numbers.[13]

In the world of the absolute contradictory self-identity, finite numbers, which are spatial and extensive, and infinite numbers, which are temporal and intensive, are described by Nishida in terms of the number formation of acting intuition: they are "through and through spatial as well as temporal, temporal as well as spatial; cardinal as well as ordinal, ordinal as well as cardinal."[14] (Here, the qualitative infinite, thought of as an intensive infinity, can be understood only as arising in their acquisition of form within the infinity of extensive magnitude ("fused with the natural numbers").

The virtual force of infinite numbers can only be grasped as a form that moves from the manifest to the manifest. The direction of Nishida's account here overlaps with his notion of a "group-theoretic world," in which individuals, while being things within the world,

---

12   *NKZ*, 10: 86.
13   *NKZ*, 10: 87.
14   *NKZ*, 10: 85.

inverse-determine" each other, interjecting the infinite in between themselves.

The Theory of Life as Poiesis

We cannot posit anything other than this world. However, this world does not consist merely of a flat juxtaposition of individuals. This world is itself an infinite nexus, while each individual expresses this nexus. Furthermore, this infinite nexus can be extracted only from the interaction between individuals, that is, within the rupture-like generation enacted by the action of individuals.

It is in the world of life that we can concretely see this absolute contradictory self-identity of the "total one" and "individual multiplicity." Life can exist only as individuals. Regardless of whether they belong to the same species, regardless of how much they resemble each other, organisms can only exist as diverging individuals creating a vast range of variations. Apart from the life of the individual, there is no such thing as the function of life. Without individuals, there would be no reality of species. It cannot be other than that everything is an individual.

By the very fact of being individual, however, individuals live as finite beings embracing the intensive infinite, containing the entire world within themselves. Neither the environment nor the world can be conceived without the mediation of the individuals that live therein. The world arises through individuals. However, this does not mean that the world is harmonious nor that the microcosm somehow expresses the macrocosm. Each individual bears the rupture of the infinite virtuality and always lives in confrontation with other individuals. Living individuals exist within a flow that always tries to become something new. To live is to bear the virtual force of recombining oneself while embracing this rupture. And living individuals try to develop this virtuality in various concrete ways by relating with other individuals just as they live through their own rupture. Furthermore, infinite virtuality can be grasped only in the function of shifting from "form" to "form." For an individual to live is to create new forms through the mediation of this kind of rupture.

In an essay entitled "Life" (1944) which is included in *Philosophi-cal Papers Vol. 7* and is one of his last works, Nishida discusses the connection between absolute contradictory self-identity and life. The basic ideas are mostly the same as what we have seen so far. It seems that here, Nishida is taking up the subject of life in order to describe the scene where the absolute contradictory self-identity arises most distinctly.

He begins by giving the following definition, which overlaps perfectly with his characterization of the individual: "a living thing is whatever exists by itself and moves by itself. Nothing else can be thought of as life."[15] The kind of life that Nishida is getting at here is not something that can be grasped in terms of vitalism, which prioritizes the total one over the individual multiplicity ("the one is many"). Life cannot be discerned anywhere other than in the divergence of materially determined individuals. Of course, nor is Nishida propounding a mechanistic theory of life, which posits only the individual multiplicity and thereby reduces the existence of life to material processes ("the many is one"). Rather, the individual multiplicity contains within its very existence the total one.

The realm of the individual, where "the one is many" and "the many is one" directly connect, is understood by Nishida as an Ouroboros-like mutual determination of the subject and world, eating its own tail:

> Our life consists in the mutual determination of the subject and environment, where the subject determines the environment and the environment determines the subject.[16]

> Life consists in the contradictory self-identity of the total one and the individual multiplicity, of the subject and the environment, of the inside and the outside; it is like the cycle of the serpent eating its own tail.[17]

As the subject of life, individuals are the bearers of life. But they do not bear life abstractly. As individuals within the environment, every living thing is singular, divergent, possesses deviations, and cannot be grasped in terms of species or historical mediation; every living thing bears life

---

15   *NKZ*, 10: 250.
16   *NKZ*, 10: 250.
17   *NKZ*, 10: 251.

as a concrete instance of becoming. In this way, individuals link their intensive forces with the extensive environment.

The environment, however, is not a factor that completely determines the life of the individual, as it cannot subsist independently of the concreteness of the individuals living within it. The environment is indeed created from the existence of individuals. And like an infinite intermingling, the created environment is again reflected within the individual. In this sense, the individual is situated within the mutual determination of subject and environment. The picture of life that results from this view of the individual can be situated in the last of the various stages of the theory of life that we have been discussing so far.

The Third Stage of the Theory of Life

Nishida's discussion of his theory of acting intuition and the theory of absolute contradictory self-identity is based twofold on the model of organic totality, the first stage of the theory of life, and on the model of place, the second stage of the theory of life. At the same time, his argument goes beyond these models and advances the discussion further.

In doing so, he re-situates intensiveness and its limit (the "transcendent" as absolute nothingness), which philosophies of life posit, back into the immanent. It is through this process of making immanent the transcendent that the aforementioned mutual nexus, wherein the biological subject (the "total one") and environmental materiality (the "individual multiplicity") define each other, is formulated. Here, there arises a world of moving life in which everything is "creator" as well as "created," "created" as well as "creator."

Let us recall that, at this stage, Nishida radicalized Bergson's philosophy of life, but at the same time he also criticized Bergson's one-sided predilection towards the intensive, arguing that the mediation of spatiality is also necessary. This was the key for describing becoming in a concrete way. Deleuze, on the other hand, at the stage where he describes becoming as it is, maintains Bergson's theoretical framework, but also breaks away from Bergsonism in one respect. Within this development, which seems to be an inevitable destination of the philosophy of life, we can discern a parallelism between Nishida and Deleuze. Let us examine this development, focusing first on how Nishida accounts for the three stages of the theory of life to then highlighting Delueze's theory of time.

In the first stage of the theory of life (organic totality), Nishida discusses the endless expansion of the individual into the totality. Here, the existence of the individual (individual multiplicity) is confirmed through its organic dissolution into an ineffable totality (total one).

In terms of temporality, this theory of relationships is deeply related to the present. At this stage, the totality is presented through the indefinite expansion of the organic nexus of the present. This is related to the mode of being of habit formation in the present. That is, at this stage the past is depicted as nothing more than a past that creates an organic nexus as a habit, together with the present. The future is likewise depicted as nothing more than a predicted future, described as a tendency created by habit. Therefore, at this stage, Nishida can only speak of a temporality connected with the present by habits. Totality is then regarded as an expansion of this kind of present (the present is posited as a fixed point and is expanded). However, this does not reflect the temporality of becoming. (In *Difference and Repetition*, Deleuze describes this as *habitus* or "habit," the first synthesis of time).

Next, in the theory of place, the second stage of the theory of life, Nishida had introduced the notion of place as a dimension different from the present, "within" which an individual exists, and attempted to factorialize the totality under which place is subsumed. Absolute nothingness was discerned as the "limit" of this factorialization. In view of temporality, Nishida's concept of place can be regarded as parallel to Bergson's pure past, which is the foundation of the present. This past subsumes the present, and yet is depicted as something different in nature from the present, and which plays the role of the foundation of the present. The pure past is, therefore, something detached from the present and has significance in its peculiar mode of being. Taken to the limit, it functions as a kind of transcendence, just like Nishida's absolute nothingness. It is thus depicted as something that provides the ontological ground of the present (in this sense, the past is said to form a circle with the present). Nonetheless, one cannot here discern the temporality of becoming. (Deleuze depicts this as "Mnemosyne" or "memory," the second synthesis of time).

In the theory of acting intuition and the absolute contradictory self-identity, however, Nishida discusses something different. At this stage, what is extracted as the realm of reality is the confrontation of individuals embracing the totality within them. Here, Nishida describes individuals that create something new while embracing a rupture within themselves, just as the part contains the whole—individuals that are truly becoming and live the eternal now. How can we depict this stage in contrast to the two earlier stages of the theory of life? Here we should consult Deleuze's discussion of the third synthesis of time.

The Temporality That Leads to the Logic of Becoming

In addition to time as an expansion of the present, which assumes an organic totality (the first synthesis of time, the temporality of habit), and the time of the past that provides its foundation (the second synthesis of time, the temporality of memory), Deleuze describes the third synthesis of time as a "time out of joint." It is depicted as the time of Thanatos, the death drive.

Here, time is presented as being linear, as an empty form. This is in contrast to the first time, which is an expansion of a point, and to the second time, which is presented as a circle. Deleuze claims that it is by mediation of this empty linearity (that is, an intensive and ordinal infinity) that a "rupture" is introduced into the present, through which the "transcendent" can enter from within. It is an infinite straight line that is assumed to penetrate the point of the present, as well as the past that forms a circle with the present by providing its foundation. This straight line that surveys eternity utilizes the fact that it is "out of joint" to create new things; it is a temporality that depicts the future. It is through the discernment of the future, which is a rupture through which the infinite intensity of intensiveness enters into the present, that one can speak of the temporality of becoming.

Deleuze, in *The Logic of Sense* (1969), which is his major work after *Difference and Repetition*, defines this third synthesis of time as the time of "Aion."[18] Yet, at the same time, he depicts the aspect of the present peculiar to the linear time of Aion as an "instant" in a sense different from the present in which the virtual is actualized. It is a kind of extensive-ization of the intensive force described as eternity.

This discussion overlaps with Nishida's notion of the eternal now. To be precise, Deleuze's arrangement in terms of the theory of time in *Difference and Repetition* has a strong tendency to highlight the time of intensiveness as virtuality, and as such, it disagrees with Nishida's logic, which describes the very intermingling of the intensive and extensive. Nor does Deleuze speak of the intermingling of the intensive and extensive as "dialectic," as Nishida does.

Nonetheless, the third synthesis of time, the time of Thanatos, is something that should be referred back to this intermingling that Nishida emphasizes. It is in the intermingling of the infinite with the finite that we can re-capture the immanence of Thanatos as death within life. And even if this intermingling is described as "dialectic," this does not mean that death and the other are merely external. Rather, it is an expression of the fact that death and the other make becoming possible in an immanent way, and hence, that life itself is infinite.

Insofar as Nishida's theme has always been the acting subject as *poiesis*, the action of this subject as an endless contradiction, and the self-moving world as becoming, it overlaps in aspiration and directionality with Deleuze's philosophy of life, which discusses the third synthesis of time as a time "out of joint." Here, the temporality that leads to the logic of becoming is exposed. And it is by this logic of becoming that we can begin to speak of life.

Nishida and Contemporary Theories of Life

How can we understand the contradictory self-identity as a theory of life itself? Let us consider this as a conclusion to "Nishida's philoso-

---

18   "Aion" refers to eternal time. Deleuze is using the term, which comes from the Greek, to express linear time as an empty form that surveys eternity.

phy of life." As we have seen, both Nishida's and Deleuze's theories of life are based on discussions of organic totality and place, but at the same time, they set out on a path that goes beyond these themes.

The force of life has always eluded physico-chemical reductionist methods, demanding a unique method of discourse. Philosophies of life have, therefore, sought a method of describing the generation of new things. The theories of Nishida and Deleuze can be situated at the forefront of these explorations. Yet some people may have doubts in some sense as to whether this way of speaking about life is legitimate. For the conception of life that has rapidly emerged in the latter half of the twentieth century is life as it is revealed by the results of molecular biology. Here, the functions of life are explicated as the functions of matter (molecules). This is the ultimate stage of the physico-chemical reduction of life. Should we, therefore, not think that the victory of reductionism is decisive?

While this view may be superficially easy to understand, it is not correct. Rather, it is the other way around. The reason for this is that molecular biology must explain why the organic world is full of such differences and diversity under the assumption that only material functions are possible, or in other words, the assumption that there is nothing in this world beyond the functions of matter. It must understand why biological phenomena exhibit such vigorous procreative power, an inclination towards unpredictable change, and the divergence of individuals that cannot be grasped in an integrated manner.

The views of holism and place may in some respects be demolished by the developments of molecular biology. It may have to rearrange the justification of its methods of discourse in a different way. However, this materialistic movement itself demands that the emergence of such phenomena characteristic of life as differentiation and diversity—that is, the divergence and generation of singular individuals—be explained. Thus, the life sciences must take on the results and issues of molecular biology and elucidate the phenomena characteristic of life in a way different from what has been done so far. In such a scenario, the life sciences would explore new methods of discourse such as self-organization and autopoiesis. This is an intellectual current shared by the various themes on life that were discussed at the end of the twentieth century.

Self-Creating Life

Theories of life today are faced with the problem of explaining how life can exhibit order in diverse ways and how it can develop itself, without positing a transcendental principle, despite the fact that there can be nothing other than the materialistic movement of the "here and now." In other words, we are confronted by the peculiar fact that the function of difference and repetition can be activated by the immanence of materiality and by this immanence alone.

We cannot neglect the connection between the developments of the life sciences and the philosophy of life. Nishida's philosophy, as well as the parallel ideas of Bergson and Deleuze, not only takes into account the various stages of the theory of life, but also presents the logic of the self-creation of life in thoroughgoing immanence, the most fundamental realm. The world as depicted by acting intuition and the absolute contradictory self-identity is a world without any transcendental principles, where there are no pre-given selves or objects, purposes or origins; it is a world of *poiesis*, where individuals hovering over nothingness define each other while containing the totality of relationships within themselves and thereby create new things.

Here, the present is not privileged as a fixed point. Nor is it subsumed into the past that is its foundation. What is presented here is a model portraying the self-creation of new things, where both the fixed point of the present and the transcendence of the past are dissolved and contained within the transition from "present" to "present."

Delineating the path of Nishida's thought may offer essential suggestions for the life sciences in thinking about the origins of life as self-creation. Because he discusses the fundamental concepts of diverging individuals and the world, virtuality and actuality, the finite and infinite, the individual and species, the logic of becoming and time, all the while taking into account each possible path of the theory of life, his philosophy may prove valuable for biological thought today. Furthermore, using life as a key concept in reading Nishida is, I believe, one way of unleashing the fundamental potential that his philosophy possesses.

There are many other topics in Nishida's philosophy that remain to be discussed. In particular, it is necessary to re-examine the meaning of his political and historical remarks from the standpoint of the individual as an intermingling of the intensive and extensive, as well as from the perspective of the theory of life. Undoubtedly, we will thereby find a new ethics that could even be called ecological, and the germs of a topic leading to a new discussion of history.

Unfortunately, there are not enough pages left to begin a new chapter and discuss these topics. For the time being, I would like to conclude by noting that our life-theoretic reading of Nishida's philosophy is a way of marking out a path whereby his texts can be made even more relevant in the future.

SUPPLEMENTARY ESSAYS

NISHIDA KITARŌ AND TAISHŌ VITALISM

The Various Aspects of the Overlap Between Nishida Kitarō and Taishō Vitalism

Let us consider Nishida Kitarō's vitalism.[1] While the role played by Nishida Kitarō in the reception of Bergson can be organized in various ways, there are at least two aspects that should be distinguished.

The first has to do with Nishida's philosophy during the period of *An Inquiry Into the Good* and *Intuition and Reflection in Self-awareness*. A major reference point in *An Inquiry Into the Good* is William James's theory of pure experience, and while the book cannot be said to be directly influenced by Bergson, it adheres closely to a very Bergsonian style of a philosophy of life. Nishida's discussion of continuity

---

1   This essay on Taishō Vitalism was originally presented at the Spring 2009 conference of the Société franco-japonaise de philosophie, as part of a symposium on the reception of French philosophy, especially Bergson, in Japan (the symposium was organized by Sadami Suzuki, Masashi Miyayama, and Tatsuya Higaki; and was moderated by Naoki Sugiyama). The essay has been largely rewritten for the Bunko edition. The original symposium presentation can be found in *Furansu Tetsugaku/ Shisō Kenkyū*, no. 14. The opening paragraph of the presentation, omitted from the present text, was as follows: "the theme of the present symposium is to examine the role played by Taishō Vitalism in the influence of Bergson in Japan. In my case, I can at least say that I have read some of the texts of Bergson and Nishida Kitarō, but with respect to the texts of Japanese thinkers of the Taishō period related to Nishida, I have not read anything more than what would allow me to give an amateur's impression (although I will refer to Hyakuzō Kurata, Ōsugi Sakae, and Hiratsuka Raichō in my presentation). However, we have Prof. Sadami Suzuki with us today, the originator of the term "Taishō Vitalism," and furthermore, the theme given to us by the moderator Naoki Sugiyama was to extract some way of re-examining the concept of life from Taishō Vitalism. As a petty reader of Bergson and Nishida myself, I am intrigued by the question of why these vitalist ideas were received in the peculiar Japanese context, what significance these ideas have, and what their limits are."

and virtuality in *An Inquiry Into the Good* and his related discussion of the differential in *Self-awareness* clearly corresponds to Bergson's division of being into virtuality and actualization, and with the logic of the differential and differenciation that Deleuze extracts from Bergson. There is a further connection between Bergson's theory of pure memory and Nishida's postulation of an infinitely multi-layered duplication model of continuity in his theory of place. However, since I have discussed this several times elsewhere, I will not repeat the details here.

The second aspect has to do with Nishida's well-known criticism of Bergson after his so-called middle period. In particular, he strongly denounces Bergson's *élan vital*, an ontological element of continuous unity and the lack of a moment of individuation in his philosophy. What is emphasized in Nishida's middle-period philosophy is, using his terminology, the "continuum of discontinuities" and the "self-determination of the eternal now," or the life that contains death, by which expressions he is illustrating the rupture of continuity and the poietic individual indicated by this rupture. These middle-period ideas (contained in the *Self-Aware Determination of Nothingness* and related texts) form the basis of Nishida's late concepts of acting intuition and the absolute contradictory self-identity. His philosophy of life can be said to head towards its unique completion by approaching Bergson and, at the same time, moving away from Bergson. Thus, while the foremost concern of his philosophy is the problem of life, I believe that he undergoes a kind of pivot with respect to his relation with Bergson. Here, we should bear in mind that it is only the middle-period Nishida that overlaps strongly with Taishō vitalism.

On the other hand, it is true that the flow of evolution and the related phenomena of life remained the focus of Nishida's thought throughout his life and, in this sense, it is necessary to discern a connection with Bergsonism. It is also a fact that the world-wide philosophical trend that made life its slogan formed a clear trajectory of thought after the nineteenth century; generally speaking, Nishida was a part of this modern current—including his love of mathematics and science—in concert with Bergson.

Let me take a detour through Bergson and explain this a bit. In the first place, what is Bergson's vitalism? From the standpoint of his representative work, *Creative Evolution*, vitalism is the idea that all existence is in some sense a continuum of life. What is emphasized above all else in the notion of continuity is temporal duration. Duration is something that is ultimate and indivisible; if it is divided, then it will turn into something else. It is something clearly distinguished from extensive, spatial phenomena. While it is not until the latter half of Bergson's life that duration is formulated as life (in *Time and Free Will* and in *Matter and Memory*, it corresponds rather to the mental existence of mind), this stance of seeing existence itself as a continuous duration or continuous change is what characterizes vitalism.

What Nishida did is to assimilate this emphasis on continuity and living duration into his discussions of the self after the pure experience period, while at the same time resisting Bergson's tendency to dissolve everything into temporal duration. Thus, he interweaves a spatial moment into temporal duration (this is the "continuum of discontinuities" mentioned above), and yet, within the *material life* that can only be discerned there, he considers *poiesis* as a becoming in a deeper way, thereby taking over Bergson's project.

I want to call this tendency (including the abuse of the differential in such ideas, as well as the structure that makes the logical treatment of virtual infinity inevitable) the "Baroqueness" of philosophy. Baroque is an art term from the sixteenth and seventeenth centuries, which emphasizes a kind of transience of reality, evanescence, and fluidity, in contrast to the idealization of fixed "eternality" characteristic of the Renaissance. It is an umbrella term for ideas that highlight the multi-layered character of reality contained within temporal change (think of Leibniz's monads), as well as the rupture-like situation where temporal change contains death (Benjamin's theory of the Baroque is closer to this direction). My use of the term is based on Sakabe Megumi's *Modernité Baroque*. Furthermore, the emphasis on the nineteenth century context is connected to the approach of Deleuze scholars such as Pierre Montebello. I believe that Baroqueness can be an extremely useful keyword, insofar as it is deeply related with the religious aspect of Nishida's philosophy (e.g., the "eternal now" and the "intuition of nothingness") and can also be used to trace contemporary versions of this aspect in thinkers like Deleuze (the eternal now is not an ideal eternity, but an eternity that fluctuates and changes here and now). It is furthermore an indicator that shows the place of Bergson and Nishida's thought within the broader philosophical context.

If we consider Nishida's philosophy in itself, however, we realize that it is very strongly influenced by Japanese views of nature. Therefore, in consideration of the global Baroqueness mentioned above, I believe it will be worthwhile to overlay Taishō Vitalism, another kind of intellectual current. There is a sense in which the significance of Nishida's thought becomes clear when we situate his texts within the tradition of Taishō Vitalism.

For example, Kurata Hyakuzō, who is today only mentioned in historical references, played a decisive role in the dissemination of Nishida's *An Inquiry Into the Good* in Japan. Kurata is a writer whose works include the play, *The Priest and His Disciples* (1918), which takes Shinran and his disciple Yuien as its subject matter. While he lived a religiously devout life, his collection of essays *Departing with Love and Knowledge*,[2] which he wrote while he was a student at the First Higher School in Tokyo,[3] and which contains writings on Nishida, became extremely popular and played the role of a kind of model for the intellectual cultivation movement of the Taishō period. As is well-known, this book is always mentioned as required reading for high school students at the time. Given that Kurata's *Departing with Love and Knowledge* played an important role in the popularization of Nishida's philosophy, we should pay attention to his reading of Nishida, regardless of its validity.

Although I referred to Kurata's work as a "popularization," the essay entitled "The Cognitive Effort of Life" included in the book clearly situates Nishida's ideas deeply within the naturalist current of the time and, in this sense, it gives a very accurate measurement of the position of Nishida's philosophy vis-à-vis vitalism. In other words, it captures the essence of Nishida's ideas.

---

2   Kurata, Hyakuzō. *Ai to Ninshiki tono Shuppatsu* (Departing with Love and Knowledge). (Tokyo: Iwanami, 2008).

3   [The "First Higher School under the old system" (旧制第一高等学校) was the first preparatory school established in Japan. It corresponds to today's University of Tokyo College of Arts and Sciences.]

In this essay, Kurata employs the term "internal life," a term which overlaps with that of the poet Kitamura Tōkoku, and writes that life "gradually differenciates and develops what is implicitly contained within itself, and our internal experience thus becomes more and more complex by the day."[4] The idea of tying together life and experience strongly suggests an attitude of emphasis on organic unity that goes beyond Nishida's pragmatic ideas. There is no denying that Kurata's reading is very accurate.

In another essay in *Departing with Love and Knowledge*, "Finding Oneself in the Opposite Sex" (the gap between this title and Nishida's theory will be examined later), Kurata discusses Nishida's famous phrase "escape from solipsism." Here, Kurata focuses on the opening passage of *An Inquiry Into the Good*: "it is not the case that there is first the individual and then experience; rather, there is first experience and then the individual." This naturalist view shows vividly what Nishida was trying to escape from. He was trying to escape from the conscious self that had been imported into Japan during the Meiji era, a self with a sufficiently modern—albeit immature—understanding of itself. It was an escape towards nature, a kind of Romanticist *nirvāṇa* into the impersonal basis of the self. We can say that, in the Taishō period, a reaction occurred against the Meiji intelligentsia who had struggled to acquire the conception of the Western ego and its rationality and the very unnaturalness of the modern ego had thereby become exposed. This reaction is, of course, strongly linked with the religious consciousness and has the tinge of a delusive expansion of the self. What Nishida calls "nature" is close to a schizophrenic, expanded self/nature, as described by Deleuze, Guattari, and Hölderlin.

This kind of reading of Nishida is, in one respect, a valid one. However, there is a certain bias in this interpretation of Nishida's philosophy. Let us consider both aspects. To understand the core of Nishida's theory of life as a dissolution of the self into nature is, in part, substantially valid. This kind of schizophrenic tendency, which we could describe as the identification of the self with the infinite, is a characteristic of the entire intellectual current of Taishō vitalism. Here, it would perhaps not be out of place to draw a connection with

---

4   Ibid., 84.

the claims of the anarchist, Ōsugi Sakae, and the pioneer of feminism in Japan, Hiratsuka Raichō.

Ōsugi Sakae is the premier anarchist of Japan. He was extremely politically active, participating in international anarchist movements and being imprisoned many times for his advocacy of socialism. He is remembered for his scandal with Itō Noe, which was a disregard of the traditional family system; ultimately, he and Itō Noe were both murdered amid the chaos that followed the Great Kantō earthquake of 1923 (this is known as the Amakasu Incident). He was a figure very characteristic of the Taishō period, but at the same time we should also pay attention to the surprising fact that his anarchist ideas were deeply informed by Taishō vitalism philosophy.

We cannot neglect the fact that Ōsugi, who was fluent in very many languages, was a translator of Darwin's *Origin of Species*, and that later, he shifted from Darwin's concept of "natural selection" towards Kropotkin's theory of "mutual aid." He had a strong obsession for theories of life and biology, unseemly for a mere social activist; he translated not only the *Origin of Species* but also Jean-Henri Fabre's *Souvenirs entomologiques*. It is certain that, at least initially, he saw in the evolution of life an emancipation from individual existence. Once evolutionary theory had been received as a theory of social evolution, it eventually began to be treated as a mere logic of the survival of the strongest. Yet, in order to understand how vitalism was conceived, it is important to realize that initially it was a theory that aspired to emancipate humans from individual existence and release into life.

Nor can we ignore the fact that "the widening of life" was one of Ōsugi's slogans: "the fulfillment of my life is at the same time an expansion of my life. And at the same time it is a widening of the life of humanity. I see in the activities of my life the activities of the life of humanity."[5] Here, Ōsugi is taking as his principle the Baroque idea of expanding the self towards the direction of life, the idea that at the same time totality (all humanity, or all life) is enfolded within the self (that life is continuously enfolded within the self). For Ōsugi, the creative instinct is itself based on an organic principle; this is an evolutionary

---

5   Ōsugi, Sakae. Ōsugi *Sakae Hyōronshū* (Collected Essays of Ōsugi Sakae). (Tokyo: Iwanami, 1996), 67.

theory of emancipation that from the outset goes beyond the subsequent social Darwinist critique of eugenics.

Hiratsuka's words, "in the beginning, woman was the sun," are also permeated by the same kind of almost simple vitalism. Needless to say, Hiratsuka is a pioneer of feminism in Japan. She founded the journal *Seitō*, and her words, "in the beginning, woman was the sun," which appeared in the first issue of the journal, had a great influence on the general public. The editorship of *Seitō* was later entrusted to Itō Noe and here also we can see how Hiratsuka's movement greatly influenced not only the political movements of the Taishō period in general, but also the post-war democratic movements for women's equality. However, the perspective of early feminism as illustrated by Hiratsuka is extremely vitalistic, essentially concerned with the nature of motherhood. Furthermore, like Kurata's reading of Nishida, it strongly aspires toward the dissolution of the modern ego (which of course is depicted as male-centered) into the direction of life:

> When we detach ourselves, latent genius becomes manifest. / We must sacrifice ourselves for the latent genius within us. / We must make ourselves egoless, as it is called (to be egoless is the limit of self-expansion).[6]

Conversely, this is related to the historical circumstance that subsequent philosophy (the major philosophies of the twentieth century, as well as Japanese thought after the early Shōwa period) plainly rejected this kind of idea of self-emancipation through self-sacrifice and instead reverted to the philosophy of consciousness, which is the exact opposite of the Bergson/Nishida kind of natural philosophy. Sakabe Megumi, who frequently uses the term "Baroque philosophy," describes the philosophy of the Taishō period at this time as a "short-lived balmy day in autumn."[7] The term "Baroque philosophy" indicates a return to a hidden lineage of thought. This is related to the criticism that maternalism in Hiratsuka's feminism is nothing but

---

6   Hiratsuka Raichō. *Hiratsuka Raichō Hyōronshū* (Collected Essays of Hiratsuka Raichō). (Tokyo: Iwanami, 1987), 21.

7   See his "Tsuka no ma no Koharu-biyori: Taishō Jidai no Tetsugaku Shisō" (A Short-lived Balmy Day in Autumn: The Philosophical Thought of the Taishō Period) in *Nihon no Tetsugaku 9: Taishō no Tetsugaku* (Japanese Philosophy 9: The Philosophy of the Taishō Period) (Kyoto: Shōwadō, 2008).

a fixation of the role of women and, therefore, fails to attain a self-conscious and equal subject.

This directly overlaps with a generalized criticism of Bergson. Various critiques of Bergson not only point out the weaknesses in his naturalist methodology, but also the fact that vitalism underestimates the significance of the domain of individual consciousness and subjectivity; it must, therefore, eventually lead to a centerless anarchism or else overlap with a correlative totalitarian conservatism. According to this critical view, there is no possibility other than these two extremes.

The same can be said about the overlap between evolutionary theory and eugenics; the maternalism characteristic of Hiratsuka has been regarded as having an affinity in one respect with totalitarian fascism. It is clear that maternalism overlaps with the idea of labor and production, encapsulated in the phrase "beget and multiply." Needless to say, insofar as post-war feminism centered on individualism—which stands in contrast with vitalism—questions the characterization of women as child-bearers, or rather, the situation in which women are characterized only as child-bearers and seeks to establish a self-conscious subject, Hiratsuka becomes in one respect an object of criticism.

Again, there is a sense in which the history of women's emancipation in the Taishō period has only been understood as a kind of momentary event or occurrence. We cannot neglect the fact that Hiratsuka's attempted double suicide in her younger years, as well as the bloody affair that resulted from Ōsugi's triangle relation involving Itō Noe (known as the Hikagejaya Incident), were both taken up as gossip magazine scandals, much like those of today. Doubtless, these kinds of actions were criticized as utterly irresponsible and eccentric order-disrupting behavior. Thus, vitalism has been criticized as nothing more than either a moral deviation that takes advantage of self-emancipation, or its reverse, a conformity to the system (one cannot help noticing how this criticism strongly resembles the way Deleuze and Guattari are generally understood).

I believe that the performance of an essentially immoral act, its political impact, and the natural antipathy towards such acts are important themes in thinking about vitalism; however, I will not go into the issue here. However, it is certain that when Bergson's vitalism was introduced into Japan via Nishida, it was read within the context of this kind of emancipation of the self into nature, and that in one respect, this essentially overlaps with an utter deviation from the order of the self. Furthermore, it is within this intellectual current of vitalism that chapter four of Nishida's *An Inquiry Into the Good* can be properly understood. For me, this was a kind of surprise. Basically, I regard Nishida's thought as the product of an extremely firm modernism. However, Nishida's vitalism in chapter four, an argument that is not as strong as it could have been, could not have been written apart from this kind of Japanese foundation; and in this sense I believe that the vitalist tradition is a more significant historical context in understanding Nishida than his Zen experiences.

Yet, at the same time, we must also pay attention to the fact that situating Nishida in this kind of context may be rather simplistic. For example, although Kurata's reading of Nishida is accurate, he only focuses on chapter four of *An Inquiry Into the Good*. In order to properly understand the continuity of pure experience, we should take into account not only the "oneness" of continuity, but also the "articulation of virtuality" that presents a schizophrenic infinitude of this kind of oneness, which is not easily handled. This logic, however, seems to be absent in both Kurata's discussions and Taishō vitalism. Yet without taking this logic into account, we cannot make clear the reason for Nishida's dynamic "revolutions" in his theory of life, and in particular, the reason why he is led to introduce the moment of the individual and the theory of *poiesis*. Nor can we avoid considering the related issue of the life-theoretic significance of Nishida's critique of Bergson.

Yet it would be too one-sided if I were to simply say that Taishō vitalism did not possess the philosophical sophistication of Bergson and Nishida, and that it, therefore, did not have much of a life in the subsequent historical development. What will we see if we take one further step into the relation between Taishō vitalism, Bergson, and Nishida?

That Which is Absent in Bergson/Nishida and Also in Taishō Vitalism

Let me summarize a bit what I have said so far. There are two aspects that should be borne in mind about the vitalism of Bergson and Nishida. The first aspect is the relativization of the philosophy of consciousness and the dissolution of the subject into a place or energy where the subject and object are undifferenciated. This aspect functions as a philosophical foundation for naturalism as a simple self-emancipation.

Yet, at the same time, an examination of the ineffability of the infinitude of the oneness and of the logic whereby this oneness bifurcates into individuals is also necessary. The question naturally arises as to why nature should differenciate into individuals.

What we should further require is that this moment of divergence of the one is not provided like a graft from the outside, or presented as an inconsistency or conflict of the kind discernable in such an account (like the infinite of the romantics). Rather, we should highlight the multiplicity contained within the one, as well as the material divergence that penetrates into the one itself. We should examine the fact that Nishida, in contrast to his conclusions in *An Inquiry Into the Good*, focused from the beginning of his reception of Bergson (*Self-Awareness*) on the role of the differential and differenciation (self-awareness is none other than the self-determination of the self which is one; it is a paradoxical and self-referential articulation involving division), and that also in his later critique of Bergson, he understood discontinuity as opposed to continuity as a spatial (place) and material (the body as acting self) moment that serves as the ground of instantaneous severance. Here, it becomes necessary to interpret the many not in opposition to the one, but as contained within the one, without appealing to a logic of contradiction. In Nishida's terminology, what is necessary is a logic according to which the one is the many, and intensive magnitude is extensive magnitude. We can thereby describe *poiesis* as a bodily practice involving moving matter by connecting temporal flow with spatial materiality (in Deleuze's terminology, we can understand this absolute contradictory self-identity as a disjunctive synthesis).

This is related to the issue of whether the naturalism of Taishō vitalism can dispel the tinge of Romanticist personalism that it displays in one respect.[8] Romanticism has the tendency to simply superimpose the oneness of the person onto the oneness of nature (that is, it is characterized by the flat overlaying of personal unity on to natural unity). Yet, when the oneness of the person is linked with the oneness of nature, it becomes necessary to take on in a schizophrenic way the infinity that fails to fit into the person. (Here, Deleuze would give Hölderlin as an example. When the infinite enters into the self, it has no choice but to take on the form of madness.)

From this standpoint, it seems that Taishō vitalism's portrayal of nature ignores too much of the self-dividing, self-differenciating moment contained within the infinitude of nature (the logic of *An Inquiry Into the Good*, chapter four is inadequate for the same reason). Normally, one cannot live in this kind of nature. Unless one thinks through this matter, naturalism will either become an anti-social machinery or adhere to a conservative tendency. The development of Bergson's theory of life by thinkers such as Nishida and Deleuze is extremely sensitive to this kind of divergence of oneness.

However, is there not some challenge that Taishō vitalism poses once more to Bergsonian naturalism, even if it is the reverse side of the weakness just mentioned? Indeed, what draws one's attention is the fact that Kurata highlights the notion of "love" in Nishida's philosophy, and does so from the perspective of the sexuality of the natural body, in a way that converges toward the idea of "sexual desire." Considering that the title of Kurata's essay is "Finding Oneself in the Opposite Sex," it is very easy to see that the theme of the emancipation and naturalization of the self leads to the theme of the body and Other as sex, that is, the theme of the natural, ecological body and its desires.[9]

---

8   It is indicative that Kurata describes Nishida's philosophy as "personalist naturalism." See Kurata, *op. cit.*, 73.

9   Related to this is the fact that the naturalist novels of writers such as Katai Tayama go into the theme of sexuality by way of making a show of one's own faults and through self-depreciating humor. Also connected to naturalism is the fact that Zola, who portrayed nineteenth century genetics in his novels, made sex as the biological nature of the body the main theme of his works. Deleuze strongly emphasizes Zola's naturalism and its relation to "genetics" in the Appendix to his *Logic of Sense*.

This is linked with the fact that when Ōsugi's vitalism (which sees in the continuity of evolutionary life the equal emancipation of humanity) takes on issues of social institution, it deals with the working body, and with the fact that Hiratsuka's maternalism (which emphasizes the sexual nature of motherhood and aims to emancipate womanhood itself at a biological level) makes its theme the child-bearer as a reproductive body. There is certainly a sense in which Taishō vitalism brings the perspective of the body as a material resource into the discussion, and does so not merely as the reverse side of a personalist ideal (from the standpoint of personalism, taking up the material body would amount to nothing more than making a show of one's own faults).

Needless to say, the body in the contexts of sexuality and labor, as a resource that bears children and can be replaced, is an important theme in contemporary biopolitical thought. But upon reflection, it is difficult to discern directly the themes of sex and labor, which should not be omitted in a consideration of the biological body, in the genealogy of philosophical theories of life from Bergson to Nishida.

In the case of Bergson, there is a strong sense in which the organism (the material body) is interpreted merely as a vestige of the *élan vital*, a mere residue of the force of diversification, so to speak. In *Matter and Memory*, the concept of the body is truncated into an abstract point that connects virtuality and actuality. And although Bergson discusses love in his later years, this love is understood merely as an opening into the infinite. He does not discuss the materiality of love.

Nishida's theory is a bit different. Nishida's theory after his middle period (as exemplified by his essay "I and Thou") embodies a revolution towards a theory of the Other—the important theme here is love towards the Other. This theory is in line with Nishida's critique of Bergson mentioned above. What is noteworthy here is that the Baroque theory, depicted as a self-vertical infinite deepening, is strongly drawn towards a horizontal poietic mutuality. This connection between the Other and the self is depicted as a revolutionary variant of the theory of place, where the self sees itself at the base of the Thou and the Thou sees the Thou in the base of the self.

This overlaps in part with Kurata's discussion of love and Hiratuska's notion of motherhood. The theory of place is clearly related with the

material body. We should also bear in mind that the way Nishida speaks
of the Other there is linked with a kind of image of pregnancy. To say
that the self contains the Thou within itself and that the Thou contains
the self within itself is plainly a thematization of the Other immanent
within the self. And this kind of immanent Other plays an important
role when Nishida takes up the body as "that which acts" and shifts to
the concept of acting intuition.

Yet love towards the Other, which Nishida describes as *agape*, is
not love towards the opposite sex as plainly described by Kurata, nor
is it agonizing over sexual desire as illustrated by Tayama Katai. However, in this case, too, it seems that the themes presented by Kurata
and Tayama are the ones that are vital for the biological body in a
more general sense I believe that Nishida was probably unable to
understand why his own thought was often superimposed on the sor-
rows of high school students like Kurata. The same can be said about
the notion of labor. While there is a sense in which Nishida's concept
of action was formulated via the stimulus of his Marxist-leaning disciples, his discussions of society are very formal.

Thus, while Nishida takes up of the body in action-theoretic terms
is effective as a critique of Bergson, we can hardly discern in him an
idea of drawing a connection between action and biological reproduction, or the related theme of emotivity. But are these not actually
indispensable themes in thinking a philosophy of life?

Why were Bergson and Nishida unable to enter into themes, despite
their employment of evolutionary theory and biological discussions?
In the case of Bergson, we should call into question the thinness of
his concept of body noted earlier, and in the case of Nishida, since the
core of his thought consists in a reassessment of practice (individuality) according to Bergsonism, it seems that there is something here
into which we can dig a bit deeper as well (various other criticisms
were probably made in the context of political philosophy).

It is not, however, my intention to merely express a dissatisfaction
with Nishida and Bergson. Rather, this will become an issue that we
should recognize and think about ourselves. For the present, I believe
the following points should be kept in mind here: (1) when the theory of life converges towards the issue of the infinite and the self, we
should think of a logic that overlays materiality onto the idea of the

infinite; (2) if we are to discern an otherness in the infinite, this otherness should not be conceived merely in terms of an ideal love, but rather we should formulate a theory that leads to the materiality (or in other words the issue of procreation) of otherness insofar as it is infinite (sexuality should not be a merely an issue of constructivism); (3) if we are to discuss the body, we should illustrate the materiality of our body, namely, the fact that it can serve as a resource for the environment and others, while highlighting the boundary between this materiality and the spontaneity of the self (that is to say, if the naturalistic situation of the self's immersion into nature is true, then we should ascertain precisely how far the naturality of the self's being extends, taking into account the scale of natural history). Insofar as the theory of life is natural philosophy, these tasks cannot be avoided. And Taishō vitalism bears significance, in that it posed these themes, which were most likely lacking in Nishida and Bergson, as issues to be considered, even if it did not do so in a sophisticated way.

Re-Connecting the Philosophy of Life with the Present

These examinations directly overlap with the issue of how we should evaluate Taishō vitalism in the contemporary context, where a new vitalism is demanded. The theme of life extracted here can be concretized more sharply by further developing it in connection with the biopolitical situation, as Foucault would say.

There was a period when similarities and connections were drawn between the fascist situation of the 1930s (the early Shōwa period) and the situation today. In some sense parallel to this, perhaps there is something we should revisit today in Taishō vitalism from a thematic standpoint, those ideas which had been depicted only in a naïve way before the tumultuous 1930s, like a "balmy day in autumn." The themes of sexuality and labor, and the questions concerning the body as a resource are indeed relevant today—these are issues that the philosophy of life ought to catch up with, as it were.

As I mentioned earlier, however, the philosophy of life has not yet fully plotted its trajectory towards this stage. In connection with the three points noted earlier: with respect to (1), the conception of a logic that overlays materiality onto the idea of the infinite, whether it be genes or egg cells and germ cells, or more recently iPS cells, the life sciences have interwoven an alternative image of the infinite into the material and productive infinity of life, an image sharper than that contemplated by Bergson and Nishida. We should take this seriously in considerations of the self, other, and time. The task here is to reformulate the body from a kind of autopoietic logic of self-organization, that is, from materiality as "moving body."

Regarding (2), the materiality of otherness, it is necessary for us to grasp the theme of love, discernable in the theories of Bergson and Nishida, as something that is itself sexual, by returning to the standpoint of the self as reproducing matter. The issue of the naturality of the body should be reconsidered as something that goes beyond the recent constructivist gender theories, as a link with natural-historical and ecological theories of the body, and fundamentally, as part of the theme of what is life in the first place. This should directly be an issue of the continuity and discontinuity of life and time.

The theme of the materiality of the body (3) is connected to the political and ethical theme of the body's self and property rights. Specifically, this theme is frequently taken up in ethical discussions of life, such as those concerning brain death, organs, and bodies with ALS. It is clear that such ethical matters should be grounded in a fundamental inquiry into the naturality and individuality of the self's and the other's body. The most important tasks are the delineation of the intimate sphere, the clarification of legal ownership, and a principled formulation of the related acts of donation and trade. The philosophy of life to come should go beyond Bergsonian and Nishidaean versions and pose a fundamental philosophy that inquires into the body as pure materiality.

From this standpoint, our evaluation of Taishō Vitalism must be extremely ambiguous. Even if Taishō Vitalism was able to thematize life as sex or labor, one can hardly say that it was able to do so in a principled manner. Honestly, I think that, if we were to present the views of Taishō Vitalism today in the context of the theory of life, it would lack impact (even if it could be characterized as a theory of life peculiar to Japan). However, if the philosophy of life as presented by Bergson and Nishida is limited, in that it cannot avoid a kind of idealization, then Taishō Vitalism can be significant in that it posed a very material theme, the issue of material emotivity. In one sense, its ideas are always alien to philosophy (during the Shōwa period, it was alien insofar as it was ignored by both political philosophy and feminism), but it is also valuable in that it continues to take up a material theme.

This overlaps with the situation today at a different level. The biopolitical situation requires us to delimit the natural-historical and environmental sphere wherein life forms its passivity as an organism and its sphere of selfhood. However, we cannot fully deal with these biopolitical issues, that is, the ineluctable naturality and materiality of the body, with an ethics or political philosophy that is utilitarian, constructivist, or dialogical (countless issues can be raised with regard to the critique of constructivist theories of gender and with natural and ecological inquiries into human instinct and institutions). The questions "to what extent are humans nature?" or "are not humans nature to begin with?" must always betray human inquiry using language. Vitalism has always acted like a poison against these healthy ideas and it will doubtless continue to do so. The historical contribution of Taishō Vitalism lies in its highlighting this poisonous aspect, which may tend to appear only as being eccentric, without brushing it aside using the word "life"—a word that often calls up a civil and lukewarm morality—and without forcing it into an agreeable theory.

LIFE AND THE DIFFERENTIAL
A Reflection on Nishida and Kuki

Introduction

Nishida wrote *Intuition and Reflection in Self-Awareness* in the Taishō period. This work contains a famous phrase "document of a hard-fought battle" in the Preface, a phrase that indicates vividly the nature of Nishida's writing.[1] It departs from *An Inquiry Into the Good* and arrives at the theory of place, which has diverse strata that cannot be encompassed by a simple account. *An Inquiry Into the Good* is a landmark text of Nishida as it highlights his account of pure experience. However, we can hardly say that the structure of pure experience in this book is well-articulated. There is a sense in which it merely illustrates in a slipshod manner the continuity of the intensive or intensive world as a realm of experience itself. In the period of *Self-Awareness*, however, Nishida begins re-examining the matter in detail from various points of view. What especially draws one's attention here, along with the Fichtean *Tathandlung* and Bergson's pure duration, is the concept of the "differential" borrowed from Neo-Kantianism, particularly the Marburg school, and the interest towards mathematics and Leibnizianism.

Nishida's discussion of the differential is, of course, directly influenced by Hermann Cohen. However, it is not merely the case that, for Nishida, the ideas of Neo-Kantianism happened to be a novel contemporary philosophy at the time. The idea of the differential is a significant insight into intensive reality. It indicates that intensive reality is differentiated and phenomenalized not by a merely extensive apparatus (that is, externally), but by the internal differences that it contains

---

within itself. Needless to say, this is related to Bergson's concept of difference that Deleuze emphasized. Insofar as the structure of self-awareness itself is linked with determination, the self-differentiating movement of the intensive, we cannot ignore this connection.

However, when Nishida later develops his ideas of place, nothingness, and absolute nothingness, the discussion of the differential recedes. The function of self-awareness itself continued to have a fundamental significance for Nishida and, as can be clearly seen in his expression "the self-aware determination of nothingness," it never lost its methodological significance during his life. Nonetheless, it is also a fact that the function of the differential, which had been employed in a characteristic way in Nishida's initial self-awareness period, is hardly treated during his multi-stratification of the discussion of place and shift to his later work. In particular, the differential is hardly taken up during Nishida's path from the discussion of absolute nothingness, which is the limit of place, to acting intuition, which is a theory of practice as a "continuum of discontinuities" that contains nothingness. As Nishida himself writes in his "Preface to the Revised Edition" of *Intuition and Reflection in Self-Awareness*, the reason for this omission lies in part in the unsatisfactory nature of the Neo-Kantian theory.[2]

Here, I want to present one contrasting example. This has to do with Kuki Shūzō's *The Problem of Contingency*. We can surmise that it was in the early Shōwa period that Kuki wrote his treatise on contingency. I do not know much about the exact relation between Kuki and Nishida. However, what draws one's attention in *The Problem of Contingency* is the fact that, in the last part of his classification of types of contingency, Kuki presents his argument clearly on the basis of the concept of the differential. In contrast to the static stage based on "contradiction" and the dynamic stage based on the "problematic,"[3]

---

2   In the "Preface to the Revised Edition" (*NKZ*, 2: 3), we can retrace the trajectory of Nishida's ideas in hindsight. Regarding the differential concept, he writes: "I have contemplated the internal unity of thought and experience, of object and act, as far as possible in terms of the Marburg school's concept of limit; but I have not been able to grasp the true, final position. Therefore, I must admit that the problem remains unsolved."

3   [Kuki uses the term "problematic" in the Latin sense of what is possible as opposed to necessarily true; see *Kuki Shūzō Zenshū 2* (Complete Works of Kuki Shūzō 2),

Kuki ultimately describes the chance that floats between being and nothingness—and the vital impetus therein—using the concept of the differential.

This constitutes two themes with respect to Kuki's relation to Nishida. The first is that for Kuki, this kind of metaphysical context overlaps with Nishida's theme of the "I and Thou." It overlaps with Nishida's middle period (early Shōwa period) discussion in *The Self-Aware Determination of Nothingness* of the "I and Thou," in connection with the themes of the "self-determination of the eternal now" and "death." Here, Nishida is illustrating the indefinite expansion of the intensiveness of absolute nothingness by interweaving it into the finite realm of the *here and now*. For Kuki, too, the multi-level nesting of being and nothingness, of life and death, forms the basis of his thought on the topic of contingency, namely, the encounter of the duality of the self and other.

The second theme is that Nishida no longer uses the term "differential" in this context. Kuki, however, continues to use the scheme of the differential at the ultimate metaphysical stage, where he deals with the birth from otherness and nothingness. This seems to be a kind of resistance against Nishida's theory. Kuki's taking up of the differential is, of course, probably influenced by Leibniz via Neo-Kantianism, but he deals with this argument in a way different from Nishida by connecting it to the themes of life and otherness. This seems to indicate a clear contrast between the two thinkers. What can we extract from this viewpoint?

Nishida and the Differential

Let us begin by covering the obvious points on the relation between Nishida's thought and the differential.[4] In *An Inquiry Into the Good*, Nishida had discussed pure experience, which forms the foundation of his original thought. It is easy to point out that this pure experience is

---

(Tokyo: Iwanami, 1980), 307.]

4   On the parallelism between contemporary French philosophy and Nishida's thought regarding the differential and the ideas that I will discuss below, see the main text of the present book.

extremely close to Bergson's idea of pure duration. Although Nishida was more heavily influenced by Jamesian pragmatism during this period, his theory of pure experience evidently shares a broad problematic with the nineteenth century philosophies around the world, including Bergson and the pragmatism connection. Nishida was certainly swimming with the tide of nineteenth century philosophy, deeply engaging with the ontology of the virtuality of intensiveness (the reality of organic continuity) and the related question of life.

There is a certain clear meaning in Nishida's shift from pure experience to self-awareness. Both pure experience and pure duration exist in the world prior to the conscious self's grasping of the world; both theories disclose the continuity of the self and world and of each phenomenon in the world. Thus, in the case of Bergson, reality is conceived as a temporal continuum that cannot be spatialized, and in the case of Nishida, it is revealed as experience itself prior to the existence of the self, understood in terms of a dynamic model where colors and smells are one.

Such theories emphasize the continuity of reality, as opposed to severed spatial phenomena. Therefore, individual phenomena (whether it be the self or the appearance of a thing) cannot be spoken of without reference to the totality that they themselves contain from the outset. In *An Inquiry Into the Good*, this situation is encapsulated in Nishida's account of God as one. The nature of the one is strongly emphasized in Bergson as well, especially in the development of his theory of life (*élan vital*). However, these theories have various problems. Even if we put aside the fundamental question of what the one is in the first place, the following question inevitably arises: in order for individual phenomena to appear, or for a self that is conscious of these phenomena to appear, is it not necessary for there to be something that carves these things out from the continuous totality? In this case, the continuity of movement and duration would be depicted as a virtual, latent reality that cannot itself be actualized. On the other hand, the phenomenal must be understood as something that differentiates itself by means of the differences (or "differentiating aspects" in Nishida's terminology) that the virtual has in itself. A logic of phenomenalization or actualization must be interwoven into the theory of intensiveness itself.

This issue, which Bergson discusses in terms of differences and actualization, overlaps with the topic of self-awareness in Nishida. Self-awareness indicates a situation where something virtual pre-existing within the totality carves out the differences contained in itself, determines itself, and becomes actualized. This kind of carving out of differences is linked to the differential. That is to say that the differential can be a very powerful tool in searching for a logic of the infinitesimal continuity of reality and the actualization of phenomena by dint of these infinitesimals. It is the differential that makes its way into the chasms of infinite reality and discloses both the invisible power existing there as well as the mechanism whereby this power differentiates into something visible.

From this vantage point, Nishida's references to the differential in his discussion of self-awareness make sense:

> Our immediate experience is the self-development of an infinite totality ... and it is the subjective act that determines the finite within this infinite. The subjective act is a process where the universal determines itself. Although I say that the subjective act determines the finite within the infinite, this function does not come from the outside. Experience determines itself ... experience can be said to be the grasping of the actual infinite (*das aktuelle Unendliche*), the seeing of the infinite within the finite.[5]

This passage shows clearly what Nishida saw in self-awareness. Whether it be Nishida or Bergson (or Deleuze), what they grasped in self-awareness and the "differential" is a system of finitizing the infinite (that which is infinite as a continuum). And if we consider consciousness as finitude, the logic of determining the infinite takes on a crucial significance. Nishida links this with the differential as follows:

> [The universal] must be something like dx in relation to x in mathematics. This is probably why the Marburg School understands the infinitesimal to be the basis of reality. Just as we regard dx as the foundation of finite x in analysis, so we perceive a given sense quality as the determination of a continuous totality....[6]

---

5   *NKZ*, 2: 56.
6   *NKZ*, 2: 57.

We can think of a finite curve as arising from an infinitesimal point; we can think of dx as the origin of x .... Can we not understand the unconsciousness that lies behind our finite consciousness as something like dx in relation to x?[7]

In terms of genealogy, this discussion of the differential comes from Leibniz via Cohen of the Marburg school. The "continuous totality" and "unconsciousness" in the above passages refer to none other than the pure experience that Nishida wanted to extract. The differential is a tool that allows us to make our way into this infinite continuity and to see the differentiation there in a form connected with its infinitesimal.

This kind of discussion shows how Deleuze appropriated Bergson's concept of difference and then developed it into the idea of the "differential." The discussion of the differential forms the basis for dealing with the system whereby the totalizing function becomes differentiated/differenciated. In *Difference and Repetition*, where Deleuze reformulates Bergson's ontology in a contemporary style, he introduces the idea of the differential, which is a very old-fashioned idea that has its origins in German idealism (such as that of Maimon). Nishida's use of the differential concept in *Self-Awareness* and Deleuze's use of the same concept in his ontological development of Bergsoninsm not only overlap in terms of subject matter (the distinguishing of intensive continuity), but are also deeply linked in terms of the tradition in the history of philosophy that they draw upon. This is a tradition that has formed the undercurrent of twentieth century philosophy, and has been forced into a minor position with the surge of the philosophy of consciousness (phenomenology) and the philosophy of language (structuralism).[8] This issue of genealogy bears

---

7   *NKZ*, 2: 86.
8   I have dealt with the world-wide development of ideas on intensiveness in the nineteenth century, albeit unsatisfactorily, in my "Introduction" to *Deleuze/Guattari no Genzai* (Deleuze and Guattari Today), eds. Suzuki Izumi, Koizumi Yoshiyuki, Higaki Tatsuya (Tokyo: Heibonsha, 2008). The question of how the Leibnizian idea that pervades Nishida, Bergson, Neo-Kantianism, pragmatism including Peirce, and the discussions on continuity in the foundations of mathematics has influenced the formation of contemporary thought around the world is an extremely interesting theme, and is also important for understanding the formation of the current of thought that includes the Kyoto School.

on the conclusion of the present essay, but I will put it aside for now. Here let us follow the development of Nishida's thought a bit further.

Nishida's Transition

As I mentioned earlier, Nishida essentially ceases referring to the Neo-Kantianial concept of the different after shifting his position. One reason for this is that because he felt a kind of dissatisfaction with the Neo-Kantian argument. However, this is also related to his questioning of the Bergsonian ontology of intensiveness itself. We can see a clear critique of Bergson in essays such as "I and Thou" and "On the Philosophy of Life," both of which are included in *The Self-Aware Determination of Nothingness*. At the basis of this critique is Nishida's fundamental doubt that the Bergonian notion of intensive magnitude sufficiently explicates the system of differenciation:

> What is truly called life is not a continuous internal development like Bergson's creative evolution, but must be a continuum of discontinuities. Only through death is life possible. The vital impetus must be intermittent.[9]

> What Bergson calls the self is merely an intuitive self and not an acting self. Bergson's self has no death; nor is it a truly living and enacting self.[10]

As is well-known, during this period Nishida frequently uses the term "continuum of discontinuities" and, in rebellion against the theory of continuous intensiveness, develops a theory that interweaves a moment of severance into continuity itself. Specifically, he presents a theory of death as eternity, represented in his essay "The Self-determination of the Eternal Now," as well as a theory of otherness appearing in the essay "I and Thou." These theories enclose within intensive experience the transcendence that absolute nothingness was able to possess. That is, they insert the infinite into the finite, thereby revealing a moment of rupture.

---

9   *NKZ*, 5: 278–79.
10   *NKZ*, 5: 346.

This has various meanings. To take one aspect, we can see here an issue of intensive magnitude and extensive magnitude that cannot be solved by relying on mere intensiveness. This serves as a fundamental doubt of Bergson's theory. That is, we cannot explain why intensive being should arise as something finite simply by saying that it undergoes a self-differentiating determination. Continuity must contain discontinuities somewhere. Otherwise, we cannot understand the necessity of intensive magnitude becoming extensive magnitude.

This is related to the fact that the late Nishida linked extensive magnitude and intensive magnitude in terms of the relation of "*soku*,"[11] using the term "absolute contradictory self-identity." Extensive magnitude is a geometrical and mutually indivisible quantity (or as Bergson would say, a quantity such that "if it were divided its quality would not change"); generally, this is represented by Cartesian space. In modern views of the history of philosophy, the quantitative is basically regarded as supporting matter or the spatial. In contrast, the intensive is something qualitative, represented by the mutually permeating flows of the sensual, emotive, and unmeasurable (or as Bergson would say, something such that "if it were divided, its quality would change"), which are usually conceived as secondary qualities in modern philosophy. Bergson regarded the flow of time as a typical case of the intensive. Against this kind of theory, which posits extensive magnitude/quantity as objective and intensive magnitude/quality as subjective, Nishida removes the boundary between the two by linking them in the relation that he calls "*soku*." At the same time, he criticizes Bergson's emphasis on only the intensive and his attempt to reduce the extensive to the intensive (thus, when Bergson speaks of life or mind, there is an echo of panpsychism), instead aiming to further logicize the domain of pure experience, where the intensive and extensive (that is, the subjective and objective) connect simultaneously. This corresponds to the fact that, in *Difference of Repetition*, Deleuze criticizes Bergson's intensiveness and formulates an intensive/extensive dynamic *spatium* and its schematism.

---

11   [A *soku* B] has the sense of "A, that is, B." It suggests that A and B are synonymous.]

In chapter five of *Difference and Repetition*, Deleuze takes up this criticism of the Bergsonian attempt at a philosophy of life that emphasizes only intensive qualities (that is, it tries to reduce space to time). Instead, Deleuze considers a realm from which quality and quantity would bifurcate and speculates about becoming from this kind of intensive space (in Nishida's terms, this would be the contradictory self-identity). This is strongly linked with Nishida's unification of space and time, including the situation of extensive magnitude *soku* intensive magnitude. For Nishida, the discussion of the body and practice begins at the stage where intensive magnitude and extensive magnitude are brought together under the relation of "*soku*."

Insofar as the body is regarded as a moving body, that is, as a subject of *poiesis*, the body must not only be material in an extensive sense, but it must also at the same time possess an intensive driving force of time—it must possess the force of becoming as its own movement. If we are to grasp the subject of becoming as moving subject, then we must above all else suppose a living matter or object in genesis. It is precisely by this moment where the intensive and extensive—that is, the temporal (becoming) and the spatial (matter)—are linked in the relation of "*soku*" that we can properly provide a discourse regarding the body; namely, that it is living matter itself and its concrete practices (although I cannot go into details here, from the standpoint of the theory of place, Nishida is from the outset more spatial than Bergson. This is connected with the fact that Nishida discussed the body and its practices in a way different from, and in some sense deeper than, that of Bergson).

Nishida's references to the differential recede in these discussions. This is indicative of a break from his earlier attempts to develop his ideas by joining Bergson and Neo-Kantianism. Kuki Shūzo, however, develops an argument that can be read as going head-on against this. In one respect, Kuki draws forth the idea of otherness embodied in Nishida's notion of "Thou." Yet he introduces the idea of the differential in a way different from Nishida. This suggests the possibility of thinking about the relation of the differential with life from an alternative perspective.

The Theory of the Differential in The Problem of Contingency

Kuki's *The Problem of Contingency* seems at first to be far removed from the sphere of Nishida's thought. Kuki's attempt to understand contingency, that whim-like situation in the *here and now*, employing extremely formalized diagrams, seems vastly different in flavor from Nishida's ever-sincere style of ontological inquiry (especially if we consider Kuki's *The Structure of Iki*, which is the aesthetic variant of *The Problem of Contingency*). However, insofar as the situation that Kuki is trying to grasp in the phenomenon of contingency is reality itself within an instant, and given that the basis of the theory of contingency lies in the "encounter" of two things that correspond to the "I" and "Thou," there is a sense in which Kuki's theory retraces Nishida's in an unexpected way. In his account, Kuki presents the topic of the differential in connection to the themes of being and non-being, all the while keeping the Neo-Kantian theory in mind (although, this consists mainly in the appropriation of Nicolai Hartmann's diagrams).

Let us begin by examining Kuki's argument. Employing an extremely formal method of exposition, *The Problem of Contingency* attempts to close in on the whim-like phenomenon of contingency and throw light upon the instantaneous reality therein. The arrangement of chapters is as follows: categorical contingency (the contingency of exceptionality possessed by individuals that defy their essence, such as four-leaf clovers), hypothetical contingency (the contingency arising from an encounter of two series, such as when a falling roof tile hits a balloon), and disjunctive contingency (a metaphysical contingency pertaining to the disjunction of being and non-being, of the form "why is this the case rather than otherwise?," e.g. "why am I a human rather than an insect or bird?"). For both Kuki and for the theory of contingency in general, the second chapter on hypothetical contingency is particularly significant.

The reason for this is that, in this section, Kuki discerns the significance of contingency in the duality of two series encountering each other. In the case of the falling roof tile hitting a balloon, there is nothing strange about the motion of the balloon as a body, or in an aging roof tile falling due to some kind of vibration. However, when these two independent series "encounter" each other, this is witnessed with "surprise" as something contingent. More broadly speaking, this is related to the issue of otherness itself; and at the same time, the topic of dualistic encounter forms the foundation of Kuki's discussion of emotivity with respect to the opposite sex in *The Structure of Iki*.

Although Kuki attempts this kind of tripartite classification of contingency, he ultimately unifies them under the metaphysical notion of disjunctive contingency. Kuki considers this using a kind of method that may be called a structural transition (that is, a recombination of the terms opposed to contingency) of the three pairs "real/non-real," "possible/impossible," and "necessary/contingent." Let me explain this briefly.

Kuki considers the first kind of contingency, the contingency of an individual that defies its essence, by overlaying it with the static situation constituted by "contradictory opposition." Here, contingency is conceived merely in terms of a contradictory relation in opposition to necessity. This relation, constituted by the law of non-contradiction and the law of excluded middle, is described as "confirmatory" and regarded as a domain where statements have determinate truth values. Whatever is contingent is an exception that cannot occur in principle.

In contrast, Kuki describes the second kind of contingency in terms of the "problematic." This is a dynamic stage of intermediacy, where contingent things encounter one another in reality. In contrast to the first kind of contingency, which was a situation conceived in terms of the statement that nothing contradictory exists, in this phase resemblance is emphasized, and the very fact that something contingent may happen is regarded as a "problem." Regarding these two standpoints, Kuki writes:

> Whether one views reality statically or dynamically is a great difference in viewpoint. If one views reality statically, then reality stands still with the quiescence of statements. ... In contrast, if one takes the standpoint of the second system and views reality dynamically, then reality will be regarded not in terms of statements but in terms of problems. Reality is something that has thickness. It is pregnant with problems. These problems must be explicated. ... Thus, insofar as reality is constituted by possibility and contingency, it explicates problems while containing within its thickness the two moments of being and non-being.[12]

---

12   Kuki Shūzo. *Kuki Shūzō Zenshū 2* (Complete Works of Kuki Shūzō 2). (Tokyo: Iwanami, 1980), 164–65.

In other words, in the first system "contingency" is opposed to "necessity" and only its impossibility or the exceptionality of its existence is noted. This is a way of looking at reality statically. In the second system, however, "contingency" is opposed to "possibility" and the real world is seen as something "problematic," as having a thickness through which the possible is explicated.

This view also overlaps with the ideas presented by Deleuze in response to Bergson. In Bergsonian/Deleuzian terms, the first system assumes a domain that ought to be described in terms of a static development, that is, it assumes phenomena that can be discerned in the plane of the present, where the differentiating forces have already differenciated. In contrast, the second system involves the becoming of reality in a dynamic sense. Just as Deleuze himself called the ideal phase brought about by the function of differentiation "problematic" (*problématique*) and conceived the movement of the difference there as "explication" (*explication*), here Kuki is dealing with a situation where reality generates dynamically.

It need hardly be emphasized that in this context, in the case of both Kuki and Deleuze, the ideas of Kant and Leibniz play a significant role. What Deleuze calls the "domain of the ideal," and what he regards as the "problematic," fall within the sphere of Kant's thought; and to say that problems are explicated is indeed Leibnizian. Kuki tentatively ascribes the static system to Kant and the dynamic system to Leibniz, but this is only for convenience. Just as in the case of Deleuze, the context in which Kuki uses Kant and Leibniz falls within the nineteenth century current of thought that links the two thinkers.

However, Kuki's originality can be seen in his ensuing discussions. Beyond the static system and dynamic system, he presents the third system as a phase characteristic of the disjunctive contingency of being and non-being. This system is formed by opposing "contingency" with "impossibility." In parallel to Kuki's illustration of the two previous systems in imitation of Kant and Leibniz, he takes up Hartmann and develops his ideas by applying the phase of contingency, which Hartmann himself did not discuss.

In this third system, at the stage that corresponds to none other than Mallarme's "throw of the die," to borrow Deleuze's expression in *Difference and Repetition*, that is, at the stage where the "fundamental "origin" of thought becomes the theme, Kuki brings out the idea of the differential. This is indicated as the transition of being and non-being at the limit, that is, as a point where the impossible comes into contact with the contingent. Here, the diagram of a circle and lines displays the differential contact between being and non-being (Fig. 1):

> Contingency is at the same time reality and nothingness. The vertex that represents nothingness *soku* reality, as the point of production, bears the power for the existence of the entire triangle. The base of the triangle expresses necessity in its state of completion, as the end-point of a developmental production. While contingency is itself an infinitesimal impossibility, by capturing an infinitesimal possibility at the peril of its fine tip, it grants the "I" to the "Thou" and receives the "Thou" under the "I," and possibilities becoming pregnant with possibilities, it finally coincides with necessity ... It is the thaumaturgy of contingency that it is able to make an impossibility, dead for eternity in non-reality and nothingness, leap towards reality (Fig. 2).[13]

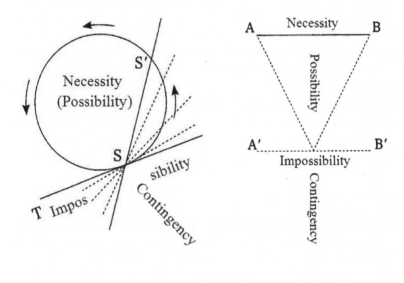

Fig. 1   Fig. 2

---

13   Ibid., 187–88.

Various themes are contained in this passage. First, the leap from impossibility to contingency, as a transition from nothingness to being, forms the core of Kuki's discussion of disjunctive contingency. It is a radicalization of the notion of contingency, which had previously been described in terms of essences and individual exceptions and dualistic encounter, in terms of the duality of being and nothingness (all the while overlaying it with the notions of primordial contingency and fate). Therefore, it very much makes sense that in his account Kuki strongly highlights the "I" and "Thou," a relation of otherness that arises by taking the framework of duality to its limit.

The combination of this subject of the "I" and "Thou" with the theme of nothingness immediately calls to mind Nishida's account of "I and Thou." After passing through absolute nothingness, Nishida's theory captures the relation of the otherness of the "I" and "Thou" by a reverse-correspondence argument (that is, it presents a reverse symmetry where the "I" sees the "I" at the base of nothingness of the "Thou" and the "Thou" sees the "Thou" at the base of nothingness of the "I"). This kind of issue of otherness, where one "encounters" nothingness, overlaps in many ways with Kuki's theory as I present it here. That is, Kuki's theory of dualistic encounter may be receptive to Nishida's theory of nothingness.

Second, Kuki is here clearly trying to introduce the notion of the differential by speaking of the circle and its tangent and the triangle and its point of contact. This is a way of firmly situating the intermingling of being and nothingness, where an infinitesimal possibility comes into contact with an infinitesimal contingency, at the core of duality. It is significant that Kuki uses the expressions "pregnant" and "production" in this connection. The theme here is none other than the arising of something from nothingness.

Let us return this discussion to its relation with Nishida's theory. Nishida's theory of the "I" and "Thou" was presented in terms of an inverse correspondence scheme, where the "I" and "Thou" see themselves in each other's base of nothingness. As such, Nishida's theory appears highly diagrammatic. In fact, considering that this model has a bearing on the issue of the acting self and *poiesis* in the absolute contradictory self-identity, we can say that it is precisely through this kind of schematism that Nishida contemplated the issue of *poiesis*.

However, to repeat, the concept of the differential has disappeared entirely from Nishida's theory here.

On the other hand, Kuki deliberately reuses the nature of the differential as a point of production in the context of the "I" and "Thou." This is a bit different from Nishida's scheme of the otherness relation between the "I" and "Thou," where the two see themselves in each other's baseless base. Rather, in Kuki's case, the theory is developed by directly superimposing the relation between the "I" and "Thou" onto the relation between being and nothingness. The metaphysical question of how something could arise from nothing is thus made to have a bearing on the issue of the differential and the Other. I believe that this theory can be examined in various ways from the standpoint of the productivity of the differential.

Life and the Other

In Nishida's inverse correspondence theory of the Other, there is a clear reciprocal phenomenon where the Other enters into the self and the self enters into the Other. The strong affinity of this scheme with a kind of psychiatric theory is vividly reflected in the works of Kimura Bin.[14] Furthermore, it need hardly be said that while Nishida goes into bodily practice at this stage, his theory is also connected with *poiesis* in the sense of tool-making. For Nishida, the context of the self and Other arises within the discussion of severance implied by absolute nothingness, the continuum of discontinuities, in connection with the union of intensive magnitude and extensive magnitude that takes the discussion of severance as its background, and it thereby leads to the theme of *poiesis*. However, what becomes somewhat diluted here is the life-theoretic perspective of production that can be expressed as a development of infinitesimal differences, that is, the idea of the birth of heterogeneity or the eruption of something new, expressed in the situation of "con-

---

14 From his earliest writings, Kimura Bin has been strongly influenced by Nishida. On the relation between the two thinkers regarding the theory of the Other, see "Jiko no byōri to 'zettai no ta'" (The Pathology of the Self and the 'Absolute Other'" in *Kimura Bin Chosakushū 2* (Collected Works of Kimura Bin 2) (Tokyo: Kōbundō, 2001).

ception" itself. This may be because, for Nishida, what was important above all else was the discussion of place and spatiality in the severance of the flow, which is predicated upon his critique of Bergson.

To repeat, I do not know much about the extent of the relation between the contents of Nishida's theory of the Other (published in the seventh year of the Shōwa period [1932]) and the theory presented by Kuki, who had been writing his book on contingency in the early Shōwa period. However, the fact that Kuki presented his theory of contingency in a thoroughly dualistic framework, superimposing it onto the question of being and nothingness that lies at the foundation of contingency, while at the same time highlighting the context of birth as substantially a vital impetus, can be read as an arrangement that stands in contrast to Nishida's philosophy of life.[15]

Of course, the duality that Kuki discusses here is not something that assumes a personal relationship between the self and Other, but rather a duality of primal contingency between being and nothingness. However, personal relationships are from the outset unequal and inhomogeneous dualities. Furthermore, the specific duality that Kuki had in mind is the relation between the opposite sexes, discussed in *The Structure of Iki* (contingency is an "encounter" with the Other). Here, duality approaches identity without being subsumed into it, while the emotivity of "iki" is depicted as the limiting situation of this kind of duality. It is quite certain that, in this notion of contingency, where birth and conception take place as a transition from nothingness to being, there is something more than mere metaphor (that is, there is a metaphysical idea) regarding the life of the body and reproduction. In any case, since Kuki's theory is itself posited as a question concerning the wonder of the fact that there is a *present* world, even if otherness possesses a transcendent absolute nothingness, it can be thought of as that which produces something at the fine tip of the *here and now* by touching at the limit that which cannot be touched.[16]

---

15   In *Shi no tanjō* (The Birth of Death) (Tokyo: University of Tokyo Press, 2008), Ichirō Mori gives an interesting account of Kuki's theory and its genesis; however, I was unable to refer to it at the time of publication of the present article.

16   This notion is strongly linked with life and reproduction, as well as the theme of otherness in considerations of life and reproduction. The issue of reproduction

This may be related to the peculiar fact that, although Nishida's thought is a philosophy of life and *poiesis*, it lacks a discussion of sexual relations and eroticism. The significance of the fact that Kuki sheds light on a theory of the differential that depicts an extremely subtle reciprocal containment of nothingness and being, which does not mesh well with Nishida's theory of the Other, may explain their points of departure.

Furthermore, taking a broader context, the theme of life and the Other may be an effective way of inquiring into the meaning of the transition from nineteenth century thought, in which the differential was discussed, to post-twentieth century thought. So far, I have pointed out the parallelisms between Nishida and Kuki, on the one hand, and the thought that leads from Bergson to Deleuze on the other. This is because I want to highlight the significance of the fact that the origins of the ideas regarding life that ought to be situated in contrast to the twentieth century philosophies of consciousness and language overlap both with the native Japanese thought of the Kyoto School and one of the currents of French postmodernism. While the Leibnizianism that comes via Neo-Kantianism directly forms a major common thread, in reality this overlap brings to light a certain heritage, a line that bores into the depths of the history of philosophy itself (or to apply an expression of Sakabe Megumi's, a Baroque tradition of philosophy that constitutes the reverse side of the canonical history of philosophy).[17] And the fact that the theme of the differential, which is related to organic production and the notion of otherness as an absolute duality are linked together in the subtle connection between Nishida and Kuki, may have links with the process of inserting an alternative arrangement of a second-person nexus into the Baroque philosophy of intensive magnitude. This only dealt with becoming in the first-person and third-person domains of the self and world.

---

contains many themes that should be discussed in depth in contemporary philosophy as problems of the *actual world*.

17   Sakabe, Megumi. *Modernité Baroque* (Tokyo: Tetsugaku Shobō, 2005). Although not directly, "Barokku no fukken wa Tetsugakushi wo dou kakikaeruka" (How will the Revival of the Baroque Rewrite the History of Philosophy," *Sakabe Megumi Shū 2* (Collected Writings of Sakabe Megumi 2) (Tokyo: Iwanami, 2006) is also suggestive in connection with this theme.

For now, I must leave open the question of how this relates to the philosophy of the Taishō period and its vitalist claims (a question that should originally have been a topic). Nonetheless, the vitalism of the Taishō period in Japan and the Baroque philosophy of life, which has a strong nineteenth century tinge, have a very intimate connection and this is a theme from which we can extract many ideas. This is a connection that has been decisively oppressed in the development of contemporary thought (in the painful process of modernization during the Shōwa period and in the case of the Taishō period ideas); and yet, it need hardly be said that its danger and, in some sense, dubiousness possess an actual significance in many ways. It is my anticipation that if, instead of restricting this circumstance to the Kyoto School, we also take into consideration the school's mutual influence with theories of the body, feminism, theories of reproduction, and theories of technology—or to use a contemporary expression, the various biopolitical contexts—then we will gain various theoretical and practical results. I will leave the task of delineating the sphere of this connection to another occasion.

POSTSCRIPT TO *GENDAI SHINSHO* EDITION

I do not have any direct or personal connections with Nishida or the Kyoto School. The aim of this book is not to restrict Nishida's texts to personal connections or the region of Kyoto, but to discern in them a momentum that dazzlingly breaks through such generational and regional boundaries. Yet there is one circumstance with respect to which I can speak of the routine topic of "Nishida and myself." It is that my high school mathematics teacher was a grandson of Nishida.

One day, that teacher suddenly told us that he had written a biography of his grandfather and encouraged anyone interested to read it. Being the impertinent high school student that I was, naturally I did not pick up the book. Back then, I had no idea that I would be so absorbed in Nishida's texts and engaged with his thought in my own research. That biography is entitled *My Grandfather Nishida Kitarō*.[1] I am afraid that I may not have been able to make sufficient use of this detailed biography in my reading of Nishida as a philosopher of life (in a sense, the orientation of the work may be radically different from my own). However, I have always kept this book in my mind as a work that clearly displays the source of the author's passion for Nishida, that is, the source of what makes Nishida appealing. The outstanding appeal of Nishida's texts must overlap somehow with his personal life, which was filled with hardship and, to use Nishida's own words, *esprits animaux* (animal spirits). And Nishida's thought, as a philosophy of life, ought to be something that maintains its spark of life as philosophy by inspiring, in one way or another, the *esprits animaux* within each one of us. I would be happy if my book has been able to transmit the vital force of Nishida's thought in some way to the next generation.

---

1   Ueda Hisashi. *Sofu Nishida Kitarō* (Tokyo: Nansōsha, 1978).

Allow me to honor the memory of that mathematics teacher, Mr. Ueda Hisashi, who has passed away.

I want to express my gratitude to Koizumi Yoshiyuki, who praised my first work on Bergson and arranged for the publication of this book; Ueda Tetsuyuki, Director of the *Gendai Shinsho* Publishing Department at Kōdansha, who accepted without any qualms my rather reckless plan to write a book on Nishida, and waited for a long time for the completion of my manuscript; and Aoyama Yū of the Editing Department, who made many corrections in my idiosyncratic writing to make it even a bit more readable. Again, I want to thank my students at the Osaka University School/Graduate School of Human Sciences, who support me by being the first to read what I write.

Tatsuya Higaki, November 2004

POSTSCRIPT TO *GAKUJUTSU BUNKO* EDITION

It is due to the effort of Mr. Ueda Tetsuyuki, who also assisted me with the *Gendai Shinso* edition, that it has been possible to republish this book, which has been out of print for some time, as a *Gakujutsu Bunko* edition with some supplementary essays. I express my deepest gratitude to him. Furthermore, since the essays were written on different occasions, there was the troublesome task of unifying the notation; and furthermore, since a new edition of Nishida's complete writings had been released, the volume number and page number references had to be rewritten. I want to thank my undergraduate and graduate students at Osaka University who helped with these tasks. I sincerely hope that this book will be of some contribution to the future of Japanese philosophy.

Tatsuya Higaki, November 2010

POSTSCRIPT TO ENGLISH EDITION

I want to thank the many people who helped realize this English translation of a book that elucidates the work of the Japanese philosopher Nishida Kitarō in relation to contemporary French philosophy. First, I want to express my gratitude to John Maraldo, Professor Emeritus of the University of North Florida, who listened to my presentation at the ENOJP (European Network of Japanese Philosophy) and encouraged me to bring out this book to the world in English. Maraldo has emphasized the importance of looking at part of the diverse possibilities of Nishida's philosophy in relation to French thought, and has even provided a foreword to the current edition. Next I want to thank Jimmy Aames, who took upon the strenuous task of translating this work. Finally, allow me to express my indebtedness to Morisato Takeshi, Roman Paşca, and Marshall Cody Staton, who recommended this translation to be published from Mimesis International's *Asian Philosophical Texts* series, and offered great help in the proofreading process.

I sincerely hope that with the publication of this book, the global simultaneity of Nishida's thought will become clearer, and that his texts will be read outside the framework of the study of a uniquely Japanese philosophy or a mere comparative study of thought.

Tatsuya Higaki, March 13, 2020

ABOUT THE AUTHOR

TATSUYA HIGAKI was born near Tokyo in 1964. He graduated from the University of Tokyo and obtained his PhD (literature) from Osaka University. He is currently a professor at the Osaka University Graduate School of Human Sciences. He specializes in contemporary French philosophy and Japanese philosophy. Apart from the current book, his works include *The Philosophy of Gambling and Contingency* [Japanese] (Kawade Shobō Shinsha, 2008), *Instant and Eternity: Gilles Deleuze's Philosophy of Time* [Japanese] (Iwanami, 2010), and *An Introduction to the Elements of Japanese Philosophy* [Japanese] (Jinmon Shoin, 2015). He has also translated Deleuze's *Bergsonism* into Japanese.

ABOUT THE TRANSLATOR

JIMMY AAMES is a PhD candidate and JSPS research fellow at the Osaka University Graduate School of Human Sciences, Japan. His main research interests are in the philosophy of Charles S. Peirce and philosophy of physics. His works include "Patternhood and Generality: A Peircean Approach to Emergence" (*European Journal of Pragmatism and American Philosophy*, 2019) and "The Double Function of the Interpretant in Peirce's Theory of Signs" (*Semiotica*, 2018). A native of both English and Japanese, he has translated numerous articles between the two languages.

Printed by
Geca Industrie Grafiche – San Giuliano Milanese (MI)
August 2020